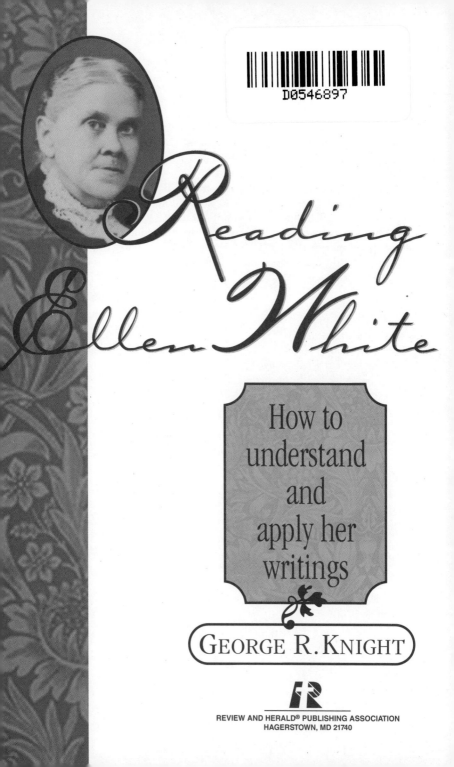

Reading Ellen White

How to understand and apply her writings

GEORGE R. KNIGHT

REVIEW AND HERALD® PUBLISHING ASSOCIATION
HAGERSTOWN, MD 21740

Bible texts credited to Phillips are from J. B. Phillips: *The New Testament
in Modern English,* Revised Edition. © J. B. Phillips 1958, 1960, 1972. Used
by permission of Macmillan Publishing Co.

Bible texts credited to RSV are from the Revised Standard Version of the
Bible, copyright © 1946, 1952, 1971, by the Division of Christian
Education of the National Council of the Churches of Christ in the U.S.A.
Used by permission.

This book was
Edited by Gerald Wheeler
Designed by Patricia S. Wegh
Cover photo by Joel D. Springer
Typeset: 12/13 Garamond 3

PRINTED IN U.S.A.

01 00 99 98 97   10 9 8 7 6 5 4 3 2 1

R&H Cataloging Service
Knight, George R.
    Reading Ellen White: how to understand and
apply her writings.

    1. White, Ellen Gould, 1827-1915—Writings.
I. Title.

                    286.732

ISBN 0-8280-1263-6

Contents

A Word to the Reader

Part One

PRELIMINARY CONSIDERATIONS

Part Two

PRINCIPLES OF INTERPRETATION

Contents

Part Three

PRINCIPLES OF APPLICATION

List of Abbreviations

AH	*The Adventist Home*
C	*Counsels on Diet and Foods*
CM	*Colporteur Ministry*
COL	*Christ's Object Lessons*
CT	*Counsels to Parents, Teachers, and Students*
CW	*Counsels to Writers and Editors*
DA	*The Desire of Ages*
Ed	*Education*
1888 Materials	*The Ellen G. White 1888 Materials* (4 vols.)
Ev	*Evangelism*
EW	*Early Writings*
FE	*Fundamentals of Christian Education*
GC	*The Great Controversy*
GW	*Gospel Workers*
HM	*The Home Missionary*
LDE	*Last Day Events*
LS	*Life Sketches of Ellen G. White*
MH	*The Ministry of Healing*
MM	*Medical Ministry*
MS	Manuscript
RH	*Review and Herald*
SM	*Selected Messages* (3 vols.)
T	*Testimonies for the Church* (9 vols.)
TM	*Testimonies to Ministers and Gospel Workers*
WLF	*A Word to the "Little Flock"*

A Word to the Reader

Ellen White's writings have been a blessing to countless thousands who have read them during the past century and a half. They have proved to be a helpful and reliable guide to those in all walks of life.

For some time there has been a need for a concise introduction to the principles of reading Ellen White. I made a first attempt at that task in *Myths in Adventism: An Interpretive Study of Ellen White, Education, and Related Issues* (Review and Herald, 1985). While that book made some inroads into the topic, its central purpose was much broader than the discussion of interpretive principles. As a result, much remained to be done. *Reading Ellen White* takes as its only purpose an examination of those principles. In the process it seeks to treat each issue of importance to the topic.

This book divides into three parts. The first deals with some general considerations, such as the purpose of her writings, their relation to the Bible, the role of compilations, and the necessity of developing a reading plan.

Part II focuses on principles of interpretation in reading Ellen White's writings. Each chapter discusses at least one important principle.

Reading and interpreting Ellen White's writings, of course, are only part of the task. The counsel also must be applied. As a result, Part III focuses on application.

Reading Ellen White has a companion volume entitled *Meeting Ellen White* (Review and Herald, 1996). That volume provides a concise introduction to the life of Ellen White, discusses her various writings, and examines the integrating themes that tie her writings together. As such, *Meeting Ellen White* is a helpful complementary volume to the present book. Combined, they provide a concise introduction to an influential Christian and to the use of her writings.

It should be needless to say that the present volume is merely an introduction to its topic rather than a comprehensive discussion. Much more could be said about the material in each chapter.

This volume does not attempt to deal with certain topics such as Ellen White's employment of literary assistants and her use of the works of other authors. Those topics and several others of like magnitude have been treated briefly in the companion volume.

I would like to express my appreciation to Bonnie Beres, who entered my handwritten manuscript into the computer; to Roger W. Coon, Tim Crosby, Paul A. Gordon, Jerry Moon, James R. Nix, Robert W. Olson, and Tim Poirier, who read the manuscript and offered suggestions for its improvement; to Gerald Wheeler and Tim Crosby for guiding the manuscript through the publication process; and to the administration of Andrews University for providing financial support and time for research and writing.

It is my prayer that this book will be a blessing to those who seek a more accurate understanding of the writings of Ellen G. White.

George R. Knight
Andrews University
Berrien Springs, Michigan

Dedication

Dedicated again to
Robert W. Olson
whose faith and love for Jesus
has made such a large difference
in my life.

Preliminary
Considerations

Part One

Chapter One

Which Is the Inspired Counsel?

In the late 1860s Ellen White wrote that "eggs should not be placed on your table. They are an injury to your children" (2T 400). Her statement seems clear enough. Yet the same author penned the following in 1901: "Get eggs of healthy fowls. Use these eggs cooked or raw. Drop them uncooked into the best unfermented wine you can find. This will supply that which is necessary to your system. Do not for a moment suppose that it will not be right to do this. . . . I say that milk and eggs should be included in your diet. . . . Eggs contain properties which are remedial agencies in counteracting poisons" (CD 204).

Now, those two bits of counsel are about as far apart as they can be. Don't eat eggs! Eat raw eggs! They represent the entire spectrum on the topic.

And yet they both came from the same author. How can that be? How could the same person give such opposite advice?

Such questions would be difficult enough if it were you or I writing. People might merely say that we were mixed up. But the ante is upped in the case of Ellen White, who claims to have counsel from God.

Did she get confused on the topic? we might ask. Or perhaps, we might reason, God changed His mind on the subject of eggs between 1870 and 1901.

In the final analysis we struggle with the question "Which statement is the inspired counsel on the topic?"

While the subject of eating eggs might seem to be a trivial issue in the works of an author who has written so much on the grand central themes of sin and salvation, the issues raised by the quotations on eggs are far from trivial. In fact, they stand at the heart of understanding inspired writers. *Reading Ellen White* seeks to help people come to grips with such issues.

The egg illustration highlights the fact that we need interpretative principles if we are to make sense out of our reading. We should also recognize that every reader of Ellen White's writings (and the writings of every other author) is already functioning with a set of interpretative principles. Even those who deny the need for the interpretation of inspired authors interpret them—in spite of themselves. Thus when they read in the Bible that "happy shall he be, that taketh and dasheth thy little ones against the stones" (Ps. 137:9), they automatically begin to understand the passage in the light of its immediate context and what they know about the love of God and God's command that His people love even their enemies (Matt. 5:43-48).

It is impossible to read Psalm 137:9 and not interpret it unless we shut down half our brain. After all, that verse hardly sounds like one of the New Testament Beatitudes—"Happy are the merciful. . . . Happy are those who make peace" (Matt. 5:7-9, Phillips). Our minds struggle to harmonize such disparate sentiments that are both in the inspired Word of God.

Similarly, we all interpret the words of Jesus in Matthew 5:27-29 about plucking out our right eye for having wayward thoughts about someone of the opposite sex. You show me a community that doesn't interpret that text, and I will show you one without eyes.

In the process of trying to make sense out of our Bibles, we develop principles for interpreting inspired materials. All of us have such principles whether we consciously recognize them or not.

The purpose of this book is to set forth some of the basic principles that we should use in interpreting the writings of Ellen White. In general, the same principles apply to the study of Scripture, even though this book is primarily concerned with her writings. As a result, most of the illustrations used will come from the pen of Mrs. White, even though I have employed some Bible illustrations where appropriate.

But, you may be thinking, *What about eggs? Which statement represents the inspired counsel?* The answer is both. Again, you may be wondering, *Which one applies to me?* That depends upon your situation. As individuals we have different physical constitutions, needs, and problems. And just as a good physician prescribes different therapies for different people with similar problems, so does God. His counsels for one person may appear to be the opposite of those given to another. That is why the readers of Ellen White's writings must do much more than mindlessly apply quotations from her pen to their lives. Readers must not only read, but read intelligently and responsibly; they must not only apply the counsel, but do so intelligently and responsibly. Unfortunately, her counsel (along with that of the Bible) can be read and applied unintelligently and irresponsibly. *Reading Ellen White* seeks to guide us in this matter by using illustrations of principles from the writings of Ellen White to make its points and, wherever possible, to demonstrate how Mrs. White interpreted her own writings.

But what about eggs? Don't worry. We will return to eggs and a host of topics of greater and lesser magnitude in the pages that follow. But first we need to consider a few general issues that will set the stage for our reading of Ellen White.

Chapter Two

The Purpose of Ellen White's Writings

U nderstanding an author's goals and intentions is central to understanding his or her writings. Readers who fail to grasp an author's purpose often seek to use his or her writings in ways for which they were never intended. Thus it is important to grasp Ellen White's self-concept of her role in the Seventh-day Adventist Church.

One of the most important things we can know about the writings of Ellen White is that they are in no way to take the place of the Bible. "In His word," she wrote in her introduction to *The Great Controversy,* "God has committed to men the knowledge necessary for salvation. The Holy Scriptures are to be accepted as an authoritative, infallible revelation of His will. They are the standard of character, the revealer of doctrines, and the test of experience. . . . The Spirit was not given—nor can it ever be bestowed—to supersede the Bible; for the Scriptures explicitly state that the word of God is the standard by which all teaching [including her own] and experience must be tested" (GC vii).

Unlike some who claim to be modern prophets and whose followers treat their writings as kind of a third testament, Ellen White explained that her function was "to exalt" the Word of

God "and attract minds to it, that the beautiful simplicity of truth may impress all" (5T 665).

She saw her purpose as bringing people "back to the word that they have neglected to follow" *(ibid.* 663). "The written testimonies," she asserted, "are not to give new light, but to impress vividly upon the heart the truths of inspiration already revealed" in the Bible *(ibid.* 665). Perhaps her most graphic illustration of her function was that she saw her writings as "a lesser light to lead men and women to the greater light [the Bible]," since they had given little heed to the Bible (CM 125).

That understanding is the most basic thing we can know about the purpose of Ellen White's writing ministry. Continually pointing people back to the Bible for authority in their Christian life, she never set forth her writings as an equal authority to the Bible or even as having any authority independent of Scripture.

It is unfortunate that some people put Ellen White's writings in a position she never intended them to be placed. Whenever people regard her writings as having more authority than the Bible, or whenever people consistently spend more time with Ellen White's writings than they do with Scripture, they are in effect using her writings to lead them away from the Bible. Those who truly grasp Ellen White's self-understanding of her mission will never make that mistake. *If people really read her writings, they will find themselves driven back to the study and authority of the Bible.*

Closely related to the point that the function of Ellen White's writing ministry is to direct men and women back to the Bible is the idea that her mission was to help people understand the principles of the Bible for their lives.

In a dream in 1871 she saw herself surrounding the Bible with several of her *Testimonies for the Church.* "You are not familiar with the Scriptures," she heard herself saying to the people. "If you had made God's word your study, with a desire to reach the Bible standard and attain to Christian perfection, you would not have needed the *Testimonies.* It is because you have neglected to acquaint yourselves with God's inspired Book that He has sought to reach you by simple, direct testimonies, calling your attention to the words of inspiration which you had neglected to obey, and urging you to fashion your lives in accordance with its pure and elevated teachings" (2T 605).

"The written testimonies," she noted in the same dream, "are not to give new light, but to impress vividly upon the heart the truths of inspiration already revealed. Man's duty to God and to his fellow man has been distinctly specified in God's word; yet but few of you are obedient to the light given. Additional truth is not brought out; but God has through the *Testimonies* simplified the great truths already given and in His own chosen way brought them before the people to awaken and impress the mind with them, that all may be left without excuse" *(ibid.)*.

On another occasion she penned that "the word of God is sufficient to enlighten the most beclouded mind and may be understood by those who have any desire to understand it. But notwithstanding all this, some who profess to make the word of God their study are found living in direct opposition to its plainest teachings. Then, to leave men and women without excuse, God gives plain and pointed testimonies, bringing them back to the word that they have neglected to follow" *(ibid.* 454, 455).

Thus far we have examined two purposes that Ellen White set forth for her writings. The first is to exalt the Bible and lead men and women to it, while the second is to clarify the great principles of the Bible for daily living so that people will have no excuse for not following its dictates. In all of this, however, she was careful to state that people did not need her writings to understand the great concepts of salvation. Her task was not to provide new or additional truths, but to simplify and magnify those already provided in the Bible.

Ellen White made the same point in another way when she wrote that "Brother J would confuse the mind by seeking to make it appear that the light God has given through the *Testimonies* is an addition to the word of God, but in this he presents the matter in a false light. God has seen fit in this manner to bring the minds of His people to His word, to give them a clearer understanding of it" (4T 246).

A third purpose that Ellen White saw for her work was to rebuke sin and to urge obedience to the Bible. That purpose, of course, is inseparably linked to the first two. "If," she counseled, "the people who now profess to be God's peculiar treasure would obey His requirements, as specified in His word, special testimonies would not be given to awaken them to their duty and impress upon them their sinfulness and their fearful danger in neglecting to obey the word of God. Consciences have been blunted because light has been set aside, neglected, and despised" (5T 667).

A fourth goal Ellen White sought to accomplish was to apply biblical principles in a modern setting, a function amply represented by the massive amount of practical counsel for everyday living found in her *Testimonies for the Church,* in the many topical compilations of her writings, and throughout her books and articles that deal with biblical themes. She claimed that "the Bible was given for practical purposes" (1SM 20). The same is true of her own writings. They do not set forth a traditional systematic theology, nor has she assumed the role of an infallible Bible commentator. To the contrary, they are practical to the utmost. Beyond rebuking sin, they point out the better way and provide guidance for daily Christian living and for the daily application of biblical principles.

Ellen White's writings not only direct us to the Bible, magnify biblical principles, rebuke sin, and provide counsel for daily living, but also point to the only solution to the human sin problem. They provide comfort by leading her readers to Jesus, to God's love, and to the plan of salvation as the only hope for a lost world. Her writings uplift the many biblical promises that culminate in the life, ministry, death, resurrection, heavenly ministry, and second coming of Jesus the Redeemer. Thus they present us with the comfort and hope of the Bible. Such writings as *Steps to Christ* and *The Desire of Ages* are her books par excellence on those themes, but we find comfort and hope throughout her writings. In uplifting the Bible she continually highlights Jesus and faith in Him as humanity's only hope.

A final purpose of Ellen White's writings that we will note is that God gave them to prepare a people for the final days of earth's history. Such books as *The Great Controversy* magnify the biblical issues that will face His last-day people. Her whole ministry aimed at not only pointing to the return of Jesus in the clouds of heaven, but also counseling men and women on the necessary preparation for that day. In that sense she echoed the mission of Christ, who urged people to be ready for His coming (see Matt. 24:36-25:46), which would be soon (Rev. 22:20). But even as she sought to make her readers ready for the return of Christ, she constantly directed them back to the Bible. Thus we read in *The Great Controversy* that "none but those who have fortified the mind with the truths of the Bible will stand through the last great conflict" (pp. 593, 594). She never tired of exalting God's Word or of pointing people to it.

We have noted in this chapter that Ellen White repeatedly described her writings as being subordinate to the Bible and as being a guide to lead believers to a better understanding of and obedience to God's Word. That subordinate role, however, does not mean that she saw her writings as lacking divine authority.

To the contrary, she repeatedly indicated that divine authority stood behind her counsel. Thus she could write: "To all who have stood in the way of the Testimonies, I would say, God has given a message to His people, and His voice will be heard, whether you hear or forbear. . . . You must give an account to the God of heaven, who has sent these warnings and instructions to keep His people in the right way" (1SM 43; see also LS 433).

Again she wrote: "You might say that this communication was only a letter. Yes, it was a letter, but prompted by the Spirit of God, to bring before your minds things that had been shown me. In these letters which I write, in the testimonies I bear, I am presenting to you that which the Lord has presented to me" (1SM 27).

Ellen White was acutely aware of her prophetic call and of her commission to guide God's people through her speaking and writing. She firmly believed that God spoke through her voice and pen in the tradition of the biblical prophets.

Chapter Three

The Relationship of Ellen White's Writings to the Bible

Y ou may be thinking that the title to this chapter sounds a lot like the content of the previous one. You're right! We are dealing with an extremely important topic that lies at the heart of a healthy understanding and a wholesome approach to Ellen White's writings. When people err on the relationship between her gift and the Bible, they have made one of the most basic mistakes possible in regard to her writings. If they are wrong on that point, they have already missed the purpose of her contribution to their personal lives and to the church and are already seriously in error as far as she was concerned. Thus it behooves us to spend a few more pages examining Ellen White's relation to Scripture.

The first point we need to emphasize is that Mrs. White did not want people making her the major authority in their lives. "Our position and faith is in the Bible," she penned in 1894. "And never do we want any soul to bring in the Testimonies ahead of the Bible" (Ev 256). That same year she set forth an identical position in relation to public preaching. "In public labor," she wrote, "do not make prominent, and quote that which Sister White has written, as authority to sustain your positions. To do this will not increase faith in the testimonies. Bring your evidences, clear and plain, from the Word of God. A 'Thus saith the Lord' is the strongest testimony you can possibly present to the people. Let none be educated to look to Sister White, but to the mighty God, who gives instruction to Sister White" (3SM 29, 30).

Again, in meeting with the General Conference leaders in 1901 to discuss the reorganization of the church, Ellen White urged them to make Bible principles their primary authority rather than her urgings and her words. In this important address to the denomination's leaders she told them to "lay Sister White to one side. Do not quote my words again as long as you live until you can obey the Bible. When you make the Bible your food, your meat, and your drink, when you make its principles the elements of your character, you will know better how to receive counsel from God. I exalt the precious Word before you today. Do not repeat what I have said, saying, 'Sister White said this,' and 'Sister White said that.' Find out what the Lord God of Israel says, and then do what He commands" *(ibid.* 33).

Such statements do not mean that Ellen White had nothing to say on the topics at hand. Nor do they imply that it is wrong to look in her writings for counsel, or that they carry no authority. Rather, the above quotations set forth a matter of priorities. Some people in each case had put Ellen White in a place she did not feel she should be. Her task was to point them to the Bible, not take its place. Those who compile dozens of Ellen White quotations on a topic but neglect their Bibles are not following Mrs. White, no matter how "faithful" they may appear to themselves. They are heading in the opposite direction from the person they claim as their guide. Ellen White consistently directed others to the Bible as the highest authority in every area of Christian living.

James White, her husband, took the same position, and so did the other early leaders of Seventh-day Adventism. In his earliest published position on the topic of Ellen's gift, written in 1847, James wrote that "the Bible is a perfect, and complete revelation. It is our only rule of faith and practice. But this is no reason, why God may not show the past, present, and future fulfillment of his word, in these *last days,* by dreams and visions; according to Peter's testimony [see Acts 2:17-20; Joel 2:28-31]. True visions are given to lead us to God, and his written word; but those that are given for a new rule of faith and practice, separate from the Bible, cannot be from God, and should be rejected" (WLF 13).

In his statement we see the delicate balance followed by several of the early Adventist thought leaders. The central idea is that the Bible is supreme, but that it indicates that God will send visions and spiritual gifts during the last days of earth's history to guide His people back to the Bible and through the shoals of the end-time crisis. Thus James White points out that Peter's use of Joel 2:28-31 in his Pentecost sermon of Acts 2 did not exhaust the fulfillment of that prophecy. God would send His Holy Spirit again at the end of time and "your sons and your daughters shall prophesy" and see visions before the Second Advent. White also quoted 1 Thessalonians 5:19-21, where Paul says: "Despise not prophesyings. Prove all things; hold fast that which is good," and Isaiah 8:20, where we read: "To the law and to the testimony: if they speak not according to this word, it is because there is no light in them" (see WLF 14).

James White and the other early leaders of the Seventh-day Adventist Church had no doubt that the Bible taught that God would pour out the prophetic gift during the last days, and that individuals had a responsibility to test those who claimed to be prophets by the Bible criteria reflected in such texts as Isaiah 8:20 and Matthew 7:15-20. Adventist leaders also had no doubt that any such gifts must be subordinate to the Bible in the life of believers, and that whenever they were not subordinated they were being used wrongly.

Thus James could write in 1851 that "the gifts of the Spirit should all have their proper places. The Bible is an everlasting rock. It is our rule of faith and practice." He went on to assert that if all Christians were as diligent and honest as they should be, they would be able to learn their whole duty from the Bible itself. "But," James noted, "as the reverse exists, and ever has existed, God in much mercy has pitied the weakness of his people, and has set the gifts in the gospel church to correct our errors, and to lead us to his Living Word. Paul says that they are for the 'perfecting of the saints,' 'till we all come in the unity of the faith' [Eph. 4:12, 13].—The extreme necessity of the church in its imperfect state is God's opportunity to manifest the gifts of the Spirit.

"Every Christian is therefore in duty bound to take the Bible as a perfect rule of faith and duty. He should pray fervently to be aided by the Holy Spirit in searching the Scriptures for the whole truth, and for his whole duty. He is not at liberty to turn from them to learn his duty through any of the gifts. We say that the very moment he does, he places the gifts in a wrong place, and takes an extremely dangerous position. The Word should be in front, and the eye of the church should be placed upon it, as the rule to walk by, and the fountain of wisdom, from which to learn duty in 'all good works.' But if a portion of the church err from the truths of the Bible, and become weak, and sickly, and the flock become scattered, so that it seems necessary for God to employ the gifts of the Spirit to correct, revive and heal the erring, we should let him work" (RH, Apr. 21, 1851).

In a similar vein in 1868 James White cautioned the believers to "let the gifts have their proper place in the church. God has never set them in the very front, and commanded us to look to them to lead us in the path of truth, and the way to Heaven. His word He has magnified. The Scriptures of the Old and New Testament are man's lamp to light up his path to the kingdom. Follow that. But if you err from Bible truth, and are in danger of being lost, it may be that God will in the time of his choice correct you [through the gifts], and bring you back to the Bible" (*ibid.,* Feb. 25, 1868).

Thus we see that James was in harmony with his wife on the place of her spiritual gift in relation to the Bible. That position also reflected the consensus of other early Seventh-day Adventist leaders. It would be hard to improve on the clarity of his words on the topic.

At this juncture it is important to recognize that just because Ellen White, her husband, and the other Adventist leaders believed that her gift of prophecy was subordinate to the authority of the Bible, that did not mean that they held her inspiration to be of a lesser quality than that of the Bible writers. To the contrary, they believed that the same Voice of authority that spoke through the Bible prophets also communicated through her.

We find a careful balance here. Even though Adventists viewed her inspiration as being equally divine in origin with that of the Bible writers, they did not see her as being the same in authority. Ellen White and her fellow Adventists held that her authority was *derived* from the Bible and thus could not be equal to it.

As a result, her authority was not to transcend or contradict the boundaries of truth set forth in the Bible. As Ellen White so aptly put it, "the written testimonies are not to give new light, but to impress vividly upon the heart the truths of inspiration already revealed [in the Bible]. . . . Additional truth is not brought out; but God has through the *Testimonies* simplified the great truths already given" (5T 665).

Unfortunately, some pay no attention to the limitations Ellen White set forth in her own writings. Such people through defective methods of interpretation (to be discussed later in this book) and faulty emphases push her ideas beyond the realm of Scripture. Their "new" and "advanced" light at times not only contradicts the Bible, but is out of harmony with the basic boundaries set forth by Ellen White herself for the use of her writings. Our only safety is to read her within the context of the biblical framework. We do well to be cautious about trying to use Ellen White to emphasize teachings not plainly taught in Scripture. Also we need to remember that everything necessary for salvation already appears in the Bible.

Before moving away from the topic of Ellen White's relationship to the Bible, we need to examine one more issue. Some Adventists have seen Ellen White as an infallible Bible commentator in the sense that we should use her writings to settle the meaning of Scripture. Thus one of the denomination's leading editors could write in the *Review and Herald* in 1946 that "the writings of Ellen G. White constitute a great commentary on the Scriptures." He went on to point out that they were unlike other commentaries in that they were "inspired commentaries, motivated by the promptings of the Holy Spirit, and this places them in a separate and distinct class, far above all other commentaries" (RH, June 9, 1946).

While Ellen White claimed that she wrote from the vantage point of one enlightened by the Holy Spirit, she did not claim that we should take her writings as the final word on the meaning of Scripture. By way of contrast, A. T. Jones, in an 1894 article on the purpose of Ellen White's writings, put them forth as an "infallible" interpreter of the Bible. He claimed that the proper use of Ellen White's writings was "to study the Bible *through them.*" Such an approach, he suggested, "will make us all 'mighty in the Scriptures'" (HM Extra, December 1894). Jones's suggestions set the course for many twentieth-century Adventists.

At this point it is absolutely essential to recognize that Ellen White rejected the infallible commentator approach to the use of her writings. The two best illustrations of that fact are her responses to the struggles over the interpretation of the law in Galatians and the identity of the "daily" of Daniel 8—theological struggles that divided the denomination's leading thinkers for the better part of three decades.

Both struggles waged around her supposed interpretation of the respective Bible passages. According to certain of her readers, she had set forth the law in Galatians as the ceremonial law in a testimony penned in the 1850s. To those individuals it was iron-clad proof as to the identity of the law. But their solution had a problem. The testimony in question had been lost, and thus the "proof" was less than conclusive.

Ellen White's response to this theological crisis is insightful. On October 24, 1888, she indicated to the contending delegates at the Minneapolis General Conference session that it was providential that she had lost the testimony in which she had purportedly resolved the issue once and for all in the 1850s. "God," she asserted, "has a purpose in this. He wants us to go to the Bible and get the Scripture evidence" (1888 Materials 153). In other words, she was more interested in what the Bible had to say on the subject than in what she had written.

But the delegates had her published *Sketches From the Life of Paul* (1883), which definitely seemed to put her seal of approval on the ceremonial law interpretation.

What was Ellen White's reaction to that use of her writings? The very day that someone brought forth the argument from *Sketches* she told the delegates, "I cannot take my position on either side [of the Galatians issue] until I have studied the question" *(ibid.)*. In short, she rejected the approach of those who would use her as an infallible commentator. We see the heart of her overall response indicated when she told the delegates, "If you will search the Scriptures on your knees, then you will know them and you will be able to give to every man that asketh you a reason of the hope that is within you" *(ibid.* 152).

Mrs. White took the same position 20 years later during the controversy over the identity of the daily of Daniel 8. In that struggle, those who advocated the older interpretation held that the new one would subvert the denomination's theology because a statement in Ellen White's *Early Writings* supported the traditional Adventist interpretation. The leader of those advocating the older interpretation argued that to make any change in the established position would undermine Mrs. White's authority. He was quite explicit on his view of the relation of her writings to the Bible. "We ought to understand such expressions by the aid of the Spirit of Prophecy [i.e., Ellen White's writings]. . . . For this purpose the Spirit of Prophecy comes to us. . . . All points are to be solved" in that manner (S. N. Haskell to W. W. Prescott, Nov. 15, 1907).

Ellen White disagreed with the argument. She requested that her writings "not be used" to settle the issue. "I entreat of Elders H, I, J, and others of our leading brethren, that they make no reference to my writings to sustain their views of 'the daily.' . . . I cannot consent that any of my writings shall be taken as settling this matter. . . . I have had no instruction on the point under discussion" (1SM 164).

Thus in both the struggles over the daily and the law in Galatians, Ellen White took the position that her comments were not to be used if she were an infallible commentator to settle the meaning of the Bible.

W. C. White also provides us with an interesting insight into the issue of his mother's relationship to the Bible. "Some of our brethren," he wrote, "are much surprised and disappointed because Mother does not write something decisive that will settle the question as to what is the 'daily' and thus bring an end to the present disagreement. At times I have hoped for this, but as I have seen that God has not seen fit to settle the matter by a revelation thru His messenger, I have come more and more to believe that it was the will of God that a thorough study should be made of the Bible and history, till a clear understanding of the truth was gained" (W. C. White to P. T. Magan, July 31, 1910).

Her refusal to function as an infallible Bible commentator should not have surprised anyone. She had not assumed that role in the past, but had always pointed people to their need to study the Bible for themselves. Never did she take the position that "you must let *me* tell you what the Bible really means." The last thing that Ellen White wanted was to get between people and the Bible.

Fritz Guy illustrates the issue nicely: "If I point toward the ceiling with my finger and say 'Look!' I do not want you to look at my finger. I want you to look *with* my finger—to look in the direction it is pointing. Indeed, if you insist on looking at my finger, I will know that you didn't understand me" (Fritz Guy, unpublished MS, Jan. 18, 1986). So it is with Ellen White. She consistently directed her readers to the Bible, but she had no intention of presenting the final word on the meaning of Scripture. In fact, in her own writing she didn't always draw the same lesson or interpretation from the same biblical passage.

Those who would make Ellen White into an infallible commentator on the Bible depart from her own counsel and in effect reverse her words and make her into the greater light to explain the Bible as a lesser light. Robert W. Olson, retired director of the Ellen G. White Estate,* explains the problems inherent in the infallible commentator approach nicely when he writes that "to give an individual complete interpretive control over the Bible would, in effect, elevate that person above the Bible. It would be a mis-

---

*In her will Ellen White established the Ellen G. White Estate, Inc., to be in charge of her literary estate. Its offices are located in the General Conference of Seventh-day Adventists world headquarters building in Silver Spring, Maryland.

take to allow even the apostle Paul to exercise interpretive control over all other Bible writers. In such a case, Paul, and not the whole Bible, would be one's final authority" *(One Hundred and One Questions,* p. 41). Our only safety is to allow the Bible writers to speak for themselves. The same goes for Ellen White. Read each writer for his or her own message in its context.

Olson hit on another important issue when he noted that "Ellen White's writings are generally homiletical or evangelistic in nature and not strictly exegetical" *(ibid.)* I. Howard Marshall helps us unpack that idea a bit more when he points out that "exegesis is the study of the Bible . . . to determine exactly what the various authors were trying to say to their original audiences," while "exposition is the study of the Bible to determine what it has to say to us" *(Biblical Inspiration,* pp. 95, 96).

How, you may be thinking, *does that apply to Ellen White's relationship to the Bible?* Simply this—Ellen White consistently pointed her readers to a study of the Bible to find out what its authors had to say (exegesis). But beyond that, she regularly applied the principles of Scripture to her time and place (exposition). In both cases she served, as she put it, as "a lesser light to lead men and women to the greater light" (CM 125). By this phrase she did not mean that she had a lesser degree of inspiration than the Bible writers, but rather that the function of her writings was to lead people to the Bible.

Having examined the important caution of not making Ellen White into an infallible commentator on the meaning of Scripture, and having recognized that she "generally" spoke homiletically rather than exegetically, it is also vital to note that she did from time to time speak to the exegetical meaning of a text. Which comments in her writings are exegetical in nature we must determine by a reading of those comments in their Ellen White context in relation to the Bible passages in question in their own contexts. Olson makes the point nicely when he writes that "one needs to be quite sure of how Ellen White is using a given text before claiming that she is interpreting the text from an exegetical standpoint for her reader" *(One Hundred and One Questions,* p. 42).

Chapter Four

Compilations: Official and Unofficial

Have we made a mistake in compiling Ellen White's thoughts on various topics into books? Doesn't a format emphasizing one quotation after another without their contexts make it easier to lose sight of principles and the larger picture?

Those are good questions. I received them during a question-and-answer session at the end of a weekend seminar I was holding in a local church on the topic of reading Ellen White. We will reflect on those questions specifically in this chapter and at various points throughout the rest of this book.

The first thing that we should note about compilations is that their creation was built into the heart of Ellen White's writing ministry. Several topical compilations, such as *Counsels to Parents, Teachers, and Students* and *Gospel Workers,* were completed during her lifetime. Beyond that, the nine volumes of *Testimonies for the Church* were put together from her letters and manuscripts. But that is not all. Even such beloved Ellen White books as *Steps to Christ* and *The Desire of Ages* are partially compilations. For example, in her preparation for *Steps to Christ* Ellen White had her secretary go through her previous articles, letters, and other manuscripts and collect those items that she could use in the new book. Of course, Ellen White was personally present to approve of the selections and the ordering of them. She was also available to add new material where needed and to modify existing documents so that the result was a smooth-flowing book.

It is important to recognize that Mrs. White never expected the compiling process to stop with her death. As she grew older she realized that she would never get all of her material into book form before her death. Her will explicitly stated that the White Estate trustees had the responsibility of "the printing of compilations from my manuscripts."

In another place she wrote that "abundant light has been given to our people in these last days. Whether or not my life is spared, my writings will constantly speak, and their work will go forward as long as time shall last. My writings are kept on file in the office, and even though I should not live, these words that have been given to me by the Lord will still have life and will speak to the people" (3SM 76).

Before we go any further in our discussion of compilations it might be best to define our terms. Those Ellen White books that we usually call compilations generally consist of large numbers of short quotations on a given subject placed in logical order and grouped into chapters by the compiler (generally the staff of the White Estate for "official" compilations). Such books as *Child Guidance* and *Counsels on Diet and Foods* belong to this category. For purposes of clarity we will call such works "topical compilations" in this volume.

The topical compilations are extremely valuable in that they tend to be encyclopedic in nature. That is, they seek to present in one place all of Mrs. White's most important material on a specific subject. Thus they are the place to look if one wants to read the spectrum of Ellen White's ideas on such diverse topics as choosing a life partner, controlling the appetite, or the Sabbath school as a soul-winning agency.

One potential disadvantage of topical compilations is that of necessity they remove most statements from their literary and historical contexts. That is significant, since the context usually helps the reader understand more fully the author's intent and complete meaning. In order to moderate that disadvantage and provide access to the context, the original source reference for each statement has been supplied in all official compilations published since Mrs. White's death. Future chapters of this book will help a person deal with some of the interpretative issues raised by topical compilations.

At the opposite end of the spectrum from the topical compilations, with their short quotations listed in encyclopedic fashion, are what most people think of as Ellen White's "books." This category includes such works as *Patriarchs and Prophets* and *Christ's Object Lessons*. As noted earlier, they also generally found their genesis in the compilation of Ellen White's previously written material. But such works had the advantage of Mrs. White's personal attention in their development. Thus she was able to write additional material as needed and modify existing statements to give such works proper balance. The "books," of course, also have the advantage of presenting their material in fuller context.

Midway between the topical compilations and Ellen White's smooth-flowing books are such works as the *Testimonies for the Church, Selected Messages,* and *Fundamentals of Christian Education.* These works generally consist of "chapter-length" selections and thus have the advantage of providing more context than do the topical compilations.

Ellen White began to publish the *Testimonies for the Church* type compilations when she realized that the counsel God had given her for certain individuals or situations also applied to many other people and situations. "Since," she penned in 1868, "the warning and instruction given in testimony for individual cases applied with equal force to many others who had not been specially pointed out in this manner, it seemed to be my duty to publish the personal testimonies for the benefit of the church" (5T 658, 659; cf. 1T 631, 632). The creation of the topical compilation format is merely an extension of that process. Thus we should see the production of additional compilations since Ellen White's death as a continuation of something that began during her lifetime.

However, compilations produced since 1915 have limitations

not present in those published before Mrs. White's death, since she wasn't available to put her final touch on them. That has made it imperative for the White Estate to set up careful guidelines and an editorial process that does its best to ensure that each book sets forth her counsel in a manner that seeks to represent its original intent and meaning faithfully.

Regrettably, those individuals and special interest groups who have a burden for one point or another and want to use Ellen White's authority to buttress their conclusions do not, in general, take similar care.

During her own lifetime Mrs. White was troubled by those who produced their own independent compilations of her statements. She was wary of all such would-be "helpers"—even those who had the best of motives and credentials. "Many from among our own people," she penned in 1894, "are writing to me, asking with earnest determination the privilege of using my writings to give force to certain subjects which they wish to present to the people in such a way as to leave a deep impression upon them.

"It is true that there is a reason why some of these matters should be presented: but I would not venture to give my approval in using the testimonies in this way, or to sanction the placing of matter which is good in itself in the way which they propose.

"The persons who make these propositions, for ought I know, may be able to conduct the enterprise of which they write in a wise manner; but nevertheless I dare not give the least license for using my writings in the manner which they propose. In taking account of such an enterprise, there are many things that must come into consideration; for in using the testimonies to bolster up some subject which may impress the mind of the author, the extracts may give a different impression than that which they would were they read in their original connection" (1SM 58).

Ellen White not only had to deal with seemingly balanced people who might inadvertently give the wrong impression through their compilations of her works, but also had to cope with excessive personalities who in one way or another used excerpts from her writings to make her say even the opposite of what she meant.

"I know," she wrote, "that many men take the testimonies the Lord has given, and apply them as they suppose they should be applied, picking out a sentence here and there, taking it from its proper connection, and applying it according to their idea. Thus poor souls become bewildered, when could they read in order all that has been given, they would see the true application, and would not become confused. Much that purports to be a message from Sister White, serves the purpose of misrepresenting Sister White, making her testify in favor of things that are not in accordance with her mind or judgment" (1SM 44).

Others in quoting Ellen White mixed in their own "filling of words" with hers and left the impression that their ideas were hers (see 6T 122, 123). Then there were those who when they "wish to strengthen their own position will bring forward from the *Testimonies* statements which they think will support their views, and will put the strongest possible construction upon them" (5T 688).

The ultimate frustration for Mrs. White must have been those who misused her writings to prove their own point either through isolated statements or through the development of personal compilations. Listen to the cry of her heart: "What I might say in private conversations would be so repeated as to make it mean exactly opposite to what it would have meant had the hearers been sanctified in mind and spirit. I am afraid to speak even to my friends; for afterwards I hear, Sister White said this, or, Sister White said that.

"My words are so wrested and misinterpreted that I am coming to the conclusion that the Lord desires me to keep out of large assemblies and refuse private interviews. What I say is reported in such a perverted light that it is new and strange to me. It is mixed with words spoken by men to sustain their own theories" (3SM 82, 83).

Ellen White, of course, could not control those who misused her writings, but she did caution that "God will judge those who take unwarrantable liberties and make use of dishonorable means in order to give character and influence to what they regard as truth" (TM 33).

And what was her advice to those who had such a strong desire to use her words to prove their points? It is plain and clear: "Let the testimonies speak for themselves. Let not individuals gather up the very strongest statements, given for individuals and families, and drive these things because they want to use the whip and to have something to drive" (3SM 286, 287).

Her solution to the issue of bringing her counsel before the people in subject matter areas in which she had not had time to develop fully into books before her death was to give the trustees of her estate the authority to make posthumous compilations of her works on various topics. She undoubtedly knew that such compilations would have their limitations, but she felt comfortable with a system that she had utilized before her death to get her works before the people. Also, she knew that such a system, with all the checks and balances and cautions built into it, would guarantee the most faithful and accurate transmission of her ideas.

In conclusion we should note that while Ellen White shied away from independent compilations during her lifetime, she also made provision for the monitored development of official compilations after her death.

In this chapter we have recognized the need for the development of compilations by the White Estate. But even with the best of care in their development, such documents can be misused. The next chapter sets forth a plan for reading Ellen White, and the rest of the book develops principles for interpreting and applying her counsel. Many of the ideas in the balance of the book will help readers relate to topical compilations in a helpful manner.

Chapter Five

Read
With a Plan

E very Christian ought to have a reading plan. Just as physical food nourishes the body, so is the spiritual side of life
fed through the "eating" (see Jer. 15:16) of God's counsel
and promises. A healthy faith is built on the firm foundation of a
knowledge of God's leading in His people's past history, a recog-
nition of His present day-by-day care, and an understanding of
His promises for the future. The primary way we gain such information is through the counsel that God has provided to His
prophets throughout the course of Judeo-Christian history.

But, you may be thinking, *there is so much to read. How do I get
started? Where shall I begin my reading?*

If we are hearing Ellen White correctly, we should begin with
the Bible rather than with her works. But even with the Bible we
need a plan. After all, if one starts in the middle of Leviticus or
Deuteronomy he or she may soon get lost in the maze of sacrifi-
cial offerings and/or ceremonial regulations.

Then again, others pick up their Bibles with a commitment
to read so much every day from Genesis right through to
Revelation. That might work for a few beginning (or even vet-
eran) Bible readers, but most (after doing fine in Genesis and the
first half of Exodus) get bogged down in the second part of

Exodus, with its meticulous descriptions of the furniture of the earthly tabernacle and the priestly garments. *Oh well, so much for reading the Bible through,* they conclude as they shut its covers.

Probably the best place to begin reading the Bible is with the four Gospels. After all, isn't Jesus and His life and death for our sins what the Bible is all about?

Thus my first suggestion is that you develop a consistent plan for reading the Gospels from Matthew through John. Get to know Jesus. Note how He related to people of all classes; capture the essence of His revolutionary teachings through His parables and sermons (especially the Sermon on the Mount); and review His promises. Don't worry about understanding everything you read. Those who have studied the Gospels all their lives still gain new insights with each reading. Just read for the blessing God has for you at your level of understanding. I might add that good modern translations will generally help such reading take on greater vividness.

When you have gone through the Gospels a few times, move on to the history of the early church in Acts. After Acts you will find a blessing from a consecutive reading of the great historical narratives of the Old Testament (Genesis, Exodus 1-20, selections from Numbers, and all of Joshua through Esther). Once again, you don't have to understand everything fully to receive a blessing.

By this time you will have read the Bible as story. Now try your hand at the New Testament letters and the Old Testament poetry, prophecy, and law. As you explore these more complex sections of the Bible, seek to relate your new understandings to the narrative that you read earlier. At this point you may be ready to read your entire Bible through from cover to cover.

Reading God's Word brings a blessing. The plan that I have suggested has worked for many. But if it doesn't fit your needs, then I would urge you to develop another program of Bible reading. But read! It's essential for your spiritual health.

Beyond the Bible, you will find additional blessing in other Christian books, including those by Ellen White. But she has written so much! Where should one begin?

My suggestion is that you don't start with the topical compilations, such as *The Adventist Home, Counsels on Diet and Foods,* or *The Retirement Years.* That is kind of like beginning to read the Bible in Leviticus. One can easily get lost in detail.

As in Bible reading, it is best to go for the big picture first. In Ellen White's writings start with the Conflict of the Ages Series. Its five volumes cover the entire period of cosmic conflict between good and evil, between Christ and Satan. And since Jesus is what it's all about, my suggestion is that Ellen White's book on the life of Christ—*The Desire of Ages*—is an excellent place to begin. You will note on the first page of most chapters of *The Desire of Ages* Bible references at the bottom of the page. They refer to the Bible passages that parallel Ellen White's treatment in that chapter. Many readers find a blessing in reading the Bible passage first and then the material in *The Desire of Ages.* From *The Desire of Ages* one could move to a sequential reading of *Patriarchs and Prophets, Prophets and Kings, The Acts of the Apostles,* and *The Great Controversy.**

Other Ellen White books that I would place at the top of my initial reading list include *Steps to Christ* (a devotional classic that could with great blessing be read before anything else she has written), *Christ's Object Lessons,* and *Thoughts From the Mount of Blessing.*

After a person has the big picture of Ellen White's writings and a "feel" for her style, burden, and overall context, then he or she will want to get into her more detailed works, into books that focus more on the application of Christian principles to specific situations. For this step in one's reading program people can either decide to go through the nine volumes of *Testimonies for the Church* or sample some of the counsel books in a field they are interested in.

Reading through the *Testimonies* offers great blessing. They address nearly every conceivable opportunity and problem in the history of the first 60 years of the Adventist movement. Readers of the *Testimonies* will find it beneficial to keep a book on denominational history (such as my *Anticipating the Advent* or Richard Schwarz's more extensive *Light Bearers to the Remnant*) and the six volumes of

---

*For a description of Ellen White's many books see chapter 5 of my *Meeting Ellen White* (Hagerstown, Md.: Review and Herald Pub. Assn., 1996).

Arthur White's biography of Ellen White handy for background reference and contextualization. Another helpful source of information on historical points is the *Seventh-day Adventist Encyclopedia*.

For those ready to venture into the counsel books after they have the larger picture in mind, I highly recommend that they read, where available, the broad-based book Ellen White developed in a particular field before they venture into the more encyclopedic topical compilations. Thus a person interested in healthful living should go through *The Ministry of Healing* before delving into *Counsels on Diet and Foods*. Likewise, those interested in education should explore *Education* before *Fundamentals of Christian Education*. Reading in that order allows one to get Ellen White's broader insights into a specific field first. Such insights will help readers to fit better the bits and pieces that they gain from the topical compilations into a balanced whole.

At this point I have one caution to urge in the reading of compilations. Remember that Ellen White gave the various counsels to many different people in many different situations. There is no way that any one reader can have all those problems. Thus readers need to be aware that the purpose of a topical compilation is to amass all the quotations on a topic in one place. Later chapters of this book will provide advice on how an individual reader should relate to the "lists" of problems, solutions, and ideals they will run across in many of the topical compilations. Meanwhile, keep in mind both the purpose of the topical compilations and their inbuilt limitations.

In conclusion, it is best for people to develop a reading plan that allows them to move progressively from the big picture to the details.

Readers will also find the four-volume *Comprehensive Index to the Writings of Ellen G. White* and the White Estate's CD-ROM disk *(The Published Ellen G. White Writings)* to be helpful for looking up various topics of interest in her writings. One final suggestion is to keep a marking pencil handy as you read. Many have found it helpful to underline the key thoughts or the central idea in each paragraph or on each page.

I would like to close this chapter with some good advice from F.E.J. Harder: "Be fair to yourself and to the author. Don't confine your reading [of Ellen White] to proof-text excerpts, 'striking statements,' isolated counsels, or illuminating paragraphs, but read her books *as she wrote them*. Of course, the compilations are excellent for reference. However, for getting acquainted with the real Ellen White, for learning what she actually taught, for appreciating what the impact of her insights can mean for your understanding, and for nurturing an experience in life enrichment, few activities can match the force of reading the inspired and inspiring writings of Ellen G. White in the literary context and form in which they came from her pen" (*What Ellen White Has Meant to Me,* ed. H. E. Douglass, p. 117).

Principles of
Interpretation

Part Two

Chapter Six

Begin With
a Healthy Outlook

Our mind-set influences our daily lives more than most people think. Those who go through life thinking everybody is out to get them find and focus their attention eventually on those who *are* truly out to get them. And those always looking for the negative in life have no trouble finding it.

Outlooks are also important in how we read Ellen White's writings. This short chapter sets forth a few suggestions that will make our reading more profitable.

First, begin your study with a prayer for guidance and understanding. The Holy Spirit, who inspired the work of prophets across the ages, is the only one who is in a position to unlock the meaning in their writings.

Beyond bringing the objective reality of the Spirit into our study, our very request also has a subjective aspect. That is, our attitude of prayer softens us and opens our minds, hearts, and lives toward a sincere desire to know God's truth and to apply it to our lives.

Second, we need to approach our study with an open mind. Most of us realize that no person is free of bias, no one is completely open-minded. We also recognize that bias enters into every area of our lives. But that reality doesn't mean that we need to let our biases control us.

To the contrary, we need to become aware of our biases and their effect on what we read and how we react to that reading. In the process we should recognize that bias comes in two flavors—bias for and bias against. Those suffering from a strong, undetected bias for an issue tend to see arguments for their topic even where they don't exist. Part of that dynamic results from wishful thinking and part from an unconscious (or not so unconscious) stretching of the facts. The same sort of dynamic takes place with bias against an idea.

While we can never completely overcome the human disposition toward bias, we can certainly recognize it for what it is and modify it. Thus part of our prayer for the Spirit is that He will help us to keep our minds open and balanced.

We might define an open mind as one that can change when faced with solid evidence. It is important that we do not come to the writings of Ellen White in an attempt to find quotations or arguments to bolster a position that we have already accepted. Such a mind-set blinds us to the facts. The only healthy way to read her writings (or those of any other writer) is with a mind searching for truth. Each of us must be willing to recognize when we have been wrong and be willing to change both our ideas and behavior as we seek to come into harmony with the full evidence.

Ellen White said it nicely when she wrote that "if you search the Scriptures to vindicate your own opinions, you will never reach the truth. Search in order to learn what the Lord says" (COL 112). She could have said the same regarding her own writings.

A third healthy mind-set in the reading of Ellen White is that of faith rather than doubt. As Mrs. White put it, "some who are not willing to receive the light, but who prefer to walk in ways of their own choosing, will search the testimonies to find something in them to encourage the spirit of unbelief and disobedience" (1SM 48).

Again she wrote, "Satan has ability to suggest doubts and to devise objections to the pointed testimony that God sends, and many think it a virtue, a mark of intelligence in them, to be unbelieving and to question and quibble. Those who desire to doubt will have plenty of room. God does not propose to remove all occasion for unbelief. He gives evidence, which must be carefully investigated with a humble mind and a teachable spirit, and all should decide from the weight of evidence" (3T 255). "God gives sufficient evidence for the candid mind to believe; but he who turns from the weight of evidence because there are a few things which he cannot make plain to his finite understanding will be left in the cold, chilling atmosphere of unbelief and questioning doubts, and will make shipwreck of faith" (4T 232, 233).

If individuals wait for all possibility of doubt to be removed, they will never believe. That is as true of the Bible as it is of Ellen White's writings. Our acceptance rests on faith rather than on absolute demonstration of flawlessness. Ellen White appears to be correct when she writes that "those who have most to say against the testimonies are generally those who have not read them, just as those who boast of their disbelief of the Bible are those who have little knowledge of its teachings" (1SM 45, 46).

The three factors we have discussed dealing with a healthy outlook are really quite closely related. A positive desire for the Holy Spirit to guide us into truth will naturally lead to openness of mind and a posture of faith. Likewise, an atmosphere of doubt leads to close-mindedness and a reticence to ask for the Spirit's guidance. It is safe to say that the fruit of our reading will depend to a great extent on the attitudes we bring to the task.

Chapter Seven

Focus on
the Central Issues

A person can read inspired materials in at least two ways. One is to look for the central themes of an author; the other is to search for those things that are new and different. The first way leads to what can be thought of as a theology of the center, while the second produces a theology of the edges.

For years I followed the second way in my reading of Ellen White and the Bible. Without thinking through the consequences of what I was doing, I began to make collections of those Bible verses and Ellen White quotations that seemed out of the ordinary, that provided "new light" that no one else had discovered or was emphasizing. In the process I often searched for the more extreme statements on the "new and different" topics I was interested in, removed them from their contexts, and formed my own compilations. After I was quite satisfied with my discoveries, my mission then was to convince fellow believers on the "advanced insights" I had culled from Ellen White and the Bible.

Unfortunately, that method of study too often creates a theology that even God can't recognize. It is a method that leads to distortions and emphases not found in the original inspired writings. Such a method prompted the founders of one of the world's fastest-growing churches to baptize living people on behalf of their dead ancestors. Noticing in 1 Corinthians 15:29 that some of the Corinthians were being baptized for those who had already died, this modern movement has elevated that concept into a central tenet of its faith in spite of the fact that such a practice contradicts the very meaning of baptism as a faith response following repentance that we find in the rest of the New Testament. That such a practice is spoken of in only one place in the New Testament, smacks of the magical, and contradicts Paul's clear teaching on salvation elsewhere should have served as a warning. It is never safe to take an obscure text as the foundation for a doctrine.

First Corinthians 15 itself treats a crucial topic in Christian theology—the reality of Christ's bodily resurrection and the resurrection at the end of time of those who believe in Him. It is an essential doctrine that stands at the heart of the New Testament. Yet some in Corinth doubted both Christ's resurrection and the future resurrection of the saints. To those with such doubts Paul responded that their faith was truly in vain if there were no resurrection and that they were of all people most confused (see verses 12-19).

That confusion extended to the practice of some of them in baptizing for the dead. If one follows the argument of the chapter, it is plain that Paul is not advocating the practice of baptizing for the dead, but asking the Corinthians why they did it if they didn't even believe at all in the resurrection of the body. Paul is merely pointing out their confusion and suggesting that their own logic should lead them to its reasonable conclusion.

To say the least, some of the Corinthians were confused about both the resurrection and baptism. Yet some in modern times have discovered what they consider new light in 1 Corinthians 15:29 and have used this isolated and obscure passage as the foundation for one of their major doctrines. A reading approach that emphasizes the different and the new leads to a theology of the edges. And such theology is often less than biblical.

The alternative reading of 1 Corinthians 15 is to examine it for its central theme. That theme runs throughout the chapter. The chapter begins with Paul telling his readers that the heart of the gospel (or good news) is that Christ died for our sins and was raised from the dead (verses 1-4). It concludes with the end-time promise of resurrection for those who have accepted the good news of Christ's death and resurrection on their behalf (verses 51-56). The chapter's central theme is resurrection, not baptism for the dead. That latter topic only provides the apostle with a back-handed illustration in which he points out the Corinthians' inconsistencies on the topic. To take the illustration and make it into a doctrine is a mistake. Yet a major church has done just that. Doing a theology of the edges may help a person arrive at "new light," but such light in the end may look more like darkness when examined in the context of the central and consistent teachings of the Bible.

One of the tragedies of many avid readers of Ellen White is that they tend to focus on reading for a theology of the edges. Mrs. White had to take a firm stand against such a use of her writings during her own lifetime. She cautioned her readers "to beware of these side issues, whose tendency is to divert the mind from the truth" (CW 47).

Again she counseled that "we should be careful how we receive everything termed new light. We must beware lest, under cover of searching for new truth, Satan shall divert our minds from Christ and the special truths for this time. I have been shown that it is the device of the enemy to lead minds to dwell upon some obscure or unimportant point, something that is not fully revealed or is not essential to our salvation. This is made the absorbing theme, the 'present truth'" (*ibid.* 49). "Satan's angels," she wrote in another connection, "are wise to do evil, and they will create that which some will claim to be advanced light, will proclaim as new and wonderful things." They are really teaching "side issues" (TM 229).

What makes the teachings of many apostles of "new light" so impressive is their obvious sincerity and the fact that much of what they have to say may be needed truth. How can we tell when we are on center or chasing stray geese near the edges of what is really important? Let's let Ellen White supply us with her answer to that question.

One significant passage on the topic appears in the book *Education.* "The Bible," she writes, "is its own expositor. Scripture is to be compared with scripture. The student should learn to view the word as a whole, and to see the relation of its parts. He should gain a knowledge of its *grand central theme,* of God's original purpose for the world, of the rise of the great controversy, and of the work of redemption. He should understand the nature of the two principles that are contending for supremacy, and should learn to trace their working through the records of history and prophecy, to the great consummation. He should see how this controversy enters into every phase of human experience; how in every act of life he himself reveals the one or the other of the two antagonistic motives; and how, whether he will or not, he is even now deciding upon which side of the controversy he will be found" (Ed 190; italics supplied).

A similar passage on the *"grand central theme"* of the Bible defines the central theme of Scripture even more precisely. *"The central theme of the Bible,"* we read, *"the theme about which every other in the whole book clusters, is the redemption plan,* the restoration in the human soul of the image of God." "Viewed in the light" of the grand central theme of the Bible "every topic has a new significance" (*ibid.* 125; italics supplied).

In such passages we find our marching orders for the reading of both the Bible and the writings of Ellen White. *Read for the big picture; read for the grand central themes.* The purpose of God's revelation to humanity is salvation. That salvation focuses on the cross of Christ and our relationship to God. All our reading takes place within that context, and those issues closest to the grand central theme are obviously of more importance than those near its edges.

It is our task as Christians to focus on the central issues of the Bible and Ellen White's writings rather than on marginal ones. If we do so, the marginal issues will fit into place in their proper perspective within the context of the "grand central theme" of God's revelation to His people. On the other hand, concentrating primarily on the marginal issues of Christianity not only leads to distorted understanding, but also creates problems as we seek to apply God's counsel to daily life. Dwelling on the marginal is the seedbed for unbalance and fanaticism.

By way of contrast, reading from the viewpoint of the "grand central theme" of Scripture helps us put everything in proper perspective. It is the way to spiritual health. It is the focal point that Jesus uplifted in the Gospels as He sought to bring the Jews of His day back to an understanding of what genuine religion was all about.

Jesus aimed at a theology of the center rather than one of the edges. He wants us to do likewise. We should not only read all of Ellen White from the perspective of the "grand central theme" of Christianity, but also read each individual book or chapter for its major contribution to our understanding of that theme. To read "Christianly" is to read from the perspective of the great controversy between good and evil, from the perspective of the cross of Christ.

Chapter Eight

Emphasize
the Important

There is quite a division in our church concerning the use of the long and the short towel in the ordinance of humility. Personally I am satisfied with the short towel; but especially with new members, there is confusion when some use one and some use the other. I would like to ask Which did Sister White herself use?

"Is there anything in her writings concerning this? (One lady claims there is something in *Early Writings.*)

"And lastly, was the use of the long towel common practice in the beginning of the Message?" (R. Shaffer to A. L. White, Nov. 1, 1933).

This letter deserves to be ranked as a classic on how to misuse Ellen White's writings. For one thing, it magnifies a topic of no biblical importance into a point of contention. Second, it tries to solve the issue by calling on Ellen White's personal example and Adventist tradition.

Perhaps the most remarkable thing about the letter is that such a congregation even had any new members to witness such confusion. It seems to me that people with good sense would stay away from such a church. And yet a disappointing number of Adventist congregations regularly feature such "sideshows."

W. C. White's answer to the letter set the matter in proper perspective. He noted that whenever his mother "engaged in the ordinance of foot washing, she used such towels as were provided by the deaconesses of the church without comment or criticism. It is my opinion that she regarded such matters as of minor importance" (W. C. White to R. Shaffer, Dec. 15, 1933).

Talk about doing a theology of the edges. The letter on the length of Communion towels is a prime example of emphasizing the "new light" of the unimportant. Yet to that congregation it had become a central issue. Thus the importance of the previous chapter, which emphasized reading for the grand central themes of the Bible and of Ellen White.

And what if Ellen White had preferred one length of Communion towel? What would that mean for the church? Nothing! It would merely have been her personal preference. Too many Adventists have tended to put Ellen White in the place of Jesus. He, not Ellen White, is our example. To shove Ellen White's example to the forefront of our religion is cultic rather than Christian. Mrs. White is in agreement with such a line of thought. Thus when some of the church leaders wanted to make her example authoritative in health reform, she said that if what she did was their authority, she "would not give a farthing for your health reform" (MS 43a, 1901). She held that their convictions needed to rest on something more solid than her personal lifestyle.

The number of candidates among biblical trivia that some want to uplift in importance is almost limitless. One example is Adventist argumentation on the issue of beards.

One document in my file lists "Fourty [sic] One Biblical Reasons Why Men Should Grow Beards." One of the most fascinating is that according to Matthew 10:30 God has numbered all the hairs on our head. Who could be so arrogant as to cut off what God cared enough to count? Another argument is that God created men with beards and it is therefore sinful to efface the image of God by shaving. Again, a man shall not wear that which pertains to a woman (Deut. 22:5), and women have bare faces. Along the same line, the article pointed out that "the effeminate shall not enter the kingdom of God." The clincher to the argument in the manuscript was that "Christ our example wore a beard."

Other individual Adventists have gotten so carried away with the topic that they have equated shaving with having the mark of the beast in the last days. "Shaving," wrote one advocate of abstinence in a document entitled "Year 1940: Another Call for the Remnant Church," "is one of the gods of this world today. . . . When you shave you are not worshipping God, but the devil. He has tried to change the Fourth Commandment; now he is trying to change the First Commandment. . . . When you try to improve upon God's handiwork, by shaving, you make a sorry mess of it, and you will have to answer for it in the very near future."

James White had tried to put the lid on the religious fascination with shaving in Adventism as early as 1857 by saying that "we must beg to be excused from taking any interest in the question, or discussing its merits or demerits in the *Review,* as we cannot look upon it as a Bible question. . . . We design to be neutral [on the subject of beards]; and neutrality, nowadays, is silence" (RH, June 25, 1857).

But winning against those with a burden in any sector of the theology of the edges is impossible. One saint later argued that James had hardly been silent on the topic of beards. Sporting one of the bushiest beards in Adventism, he had obviously voted against shaving. Such contorted reasoning is one of the hallmarks of those who build a theology of the edges by selecting stray quotations on one topic or another and applying their own form of "airtight logic" to their gleanings.

Ellen White, as might be expected, was in harmony with her husband on the topic of shaving. W. C. White penned in 1907 that "when brethren have come to her, expressing their great burden over this matter [of shaving], she has said that it would be much better for them to exercise their time and mental power in dealing with more vital questions" (W. C. White to M. Hirst, Feb. 24, 1907).

Ellen White repeatedly directed those majoring in minors back to the central themes of Scripture, especially the plan of salvation and the mission of God's people. That was so even in doctrinal areas. One example is the struggle over the identity of "the daily" of Daniel 8 that split the leaders of the denomination for more than a decade. Even though some of the agitators were using quotations from her writings to sustain their positions, she flatly said they were on the wrong track. *"The enemy of our work,"* she wrote, *"is pleased when a subject of minor importance can be used to divert the minds of our brethren from the great questions that should be the burden of our message.* As this is not a test question, I entreat of my brethren that they shall not allow the enemy to triumph by having it treated as such" (1SM 164, 165; italics supplied).

She made similar statements regarding the tussle over the identity of the law in Galatians that divided the church during the 1880s and 1890s. To her it wasn't a central issue of importance, even though certain church leaders had used her writings to give the issue prominence. She even took the same position in one of the most divisive theological controversies in modern Adventism—the one over the human nature of Christ (once again largely sustained by appeals to her writings). At the end of her most extensive treatment of the topic, she not only warned people about the danger of seeking to probe into the subject, but went on to suggest that "there are many questions treated upon that are not necessary for the perfection of the faith" (letter 8, 1895).

In her mind there are many things clearly revealed that are central to the faith and the plan of salvation. It is to those things that she constantly pointed her readers. She repeatedly counseled her readers to emphasize the important.

Thus while she *might* make remarks in the course of her advice to the church on such issues as Communion towels, shaving, or the law in Galatians, such issues were not her focal point. In like manner, when Jesus told His hearers that "the very hairs of your head are all numbered" (Matt. 10:30), His concern was not the propriety or sinfulness of shaving, but the love of God and the infinite value of every human being in His eyes. Jesus consistently emphasized the major issues of life, and He sought to lead the Jews of His day to focus on the truly important things in religion.

Taken in her full context, Ellen White did the same thing.

Before moving away from the subject of the necessity of emphasizing what is truly important in Ellen White's writings, we need to examine one more issue. It centers on the question of whether everything Ellen White wrote was inspired. What if, some may ask, some "uninspired" ideas or facts got into her writings? That question takes on added importance because Ellen White claimed God's guidance for her letters and interviews in addition to guidance in the development of her books and articles (see 3SM 50, 51).

The standard answer to that question is that Ellen White spoke and wrote about both sacred and common topics. She not only wrote family letters on "common, everyday topics" (see letters 201, 202, 1903), but also discussed common topics in her work with other people.

For example, in 1909 she recalled an experience she had had with E. S. Ballenger, former manager of the Paradise Valley Sanitarium, regarding the number of rooms in that institution. He had lost confidence in her, he claimed, because she said "the sanitarium contained forty rooms, when there were really only thirty-eight." As Mrs. White discussed the Ballenger case, she made a distinction between the sacred and the common.

"The information given concerning the number of rooms in the Paradise Valley Sanitarium was given," she noted, "not as a revelation from the Lord, but simply as a human opinion. There has never been revealed to me the exact number of rooms in any of our sanitariums; and the knowledge I have obtained of such things I have gained by inquiring of those who were supposed to know. . . .

"There are times when common things must be stated, common thoughts must occupy the mind, common letters must be written and information given that has passed from one to another of the workers. Such words, such information, are not given under the special inspiration of the Spirit of God. Questions are asked at times that are not upon religious subjects at all, and these questions must be answered. We converse about houses and lands, trades to be made, and locations for our institutions, their advantages and disadvantages.

"I receive letters asking for advice on many strange subjects, and I advise according to the light that has been given me" (1SM 38, 39).

While the distinction between the sacred and the common has been the traditional position on the topic of whether everything that Ellen White wrote was inspired, some have suggested that such a position implies that Ellen White could *never* have had any private or personal communications on religious topics or topics with religious implications. That suggestion raises an important issue in regard to both Ellen White and the biblical prophets. Were they completely overwhelmed by God to the place where they lost their religious individuality?

That question brings to mind the case of the prophet Nathan. After telling David that he was the man to build the Temple, a subsequent message from the Lord instructed him that not David but David's son was to carry out its construction (2 Sam. 7; 1 Chron. 17:1-15).

Here is a distinct case in which a prophet had a religious position on a *very important* topic with religious implications that turned out to be merely his own opinion. With that in mind, we might ask ourselves if it was impossible for Mrs. White to have personal views on religious topics that might have found their way into a private letter to a family member or friend. And given the way topical compilations are put together, what if that opinion eventually found its way into a book?

Wouldn't such a situation be problematic or even misleading? Maybe or maybe not. It depends how one reads Ellen White. That is one reason I have spent so much space in the past two chapters emphasizing the necessity to focus on the great central themes in reading inspired materials and in emphasizing the really important rather than those statements at the edges of the thought of God's spokespeople.

Anyone who reads Ellen White with any regularity soon realizes that she discussed many topics again and again in a variety of contexts. Thus those things that she was really concerned with she repeatedly treats in her writings from a number of perspectives. Such repetitions that are found throughout her writings express the burden of her message rather than those obscure, infrequently made remarks that appear to be at the edges of her thought. If one reads for the center of her message rather than its edges, the issue of the fine line between the sacred and the common loses its forcefulness. Neither do such readers have to be overly concerned with what might be thought of as the gray areas that intersect both the sacred and the common.

In summary I would like to suggest that the traditional distinction between the sacred and the common is helpful. But beyond that distinction it seems to me that it is important to focus on the central and oft-repeated themes of Ellen White's writing ministry. That second rule keeps us from overemphasizing the marginal in her writings and helps us focus on the essence of her message to the church.

Chapter Nine

Account for Problems in Communication

The process of communication is not as simple as we might at first suspect. Let me give an example from my own experience.

For several years I served as an elementary school teacher. I loved my work, but children will be children, and they can get noisy and out of hand. Early in my experience I noted certain patterns. The class would get progressively more "active," I would lay down the law, things would quiet down for a time, then the problem would build up to the point where something had to be done. Finally I would have to speak firmly and again lay down the law. Sometimes I would have to deal with the entire class. The night before the "big event" I would plan exactly how I would communicate my frustrations and desires.

The problem that I faced in such situations was the variation in student sensitivity. Every classroom had extremely sensitive children in it. All I had to do was to look crosswise at them and they came unglued. At the other end of the spectrum were the insensitive ones. I could have, figuratively speaking, hit them over the head with a baseball bat and still wouldn't have made the needed impression.

But things were bad. Something had to be done. The whole

class needed "my lecture." It was obvious that if I spoke calmly and sweetly to protect the sensitive, I would not reach those who needed more forceful treatment. The only solution was to frame my words powerfully enough so that even the most hardened would hear. The result? The weak felt crushed by my disapproval of them, while the difficult acted as if I had never uttered a word. Communication, I concluded, was more difficult than I had thought it was.

God has the same problem with His human children. They too range from the overly sensitive to the gospel hardened. Have you ever thought about how that affects His ability to communicate through His prophets?

The topic was certainly at the forefront of James White's thinking as he watched his wife struggle to lead the early Adventists down the path of reform. In 1868 he wrote that "Mrs. White needs the help of all who can help in the cause of truth and reform. The people generally are slow to move, and hardly move at all. A few move cautiously and well, while others go too fast. . . . He who sees the duty of reform, and is full strict enough in any case, and allows of no exceptions, and drives matters, is sure to drive the reform into the ground, hurt his own soul, and injure others. Such do not help Mrs. White, but greatly burden her in her arduous work. . . . *She works to this disadvantage, namely: she makes strong appeals to the people, which a few feel deeply, and take strong positions, and go to extremes. Then to save the cause from ruin in consequence of these extremes, she is obliged to come out with reproofs for extremists in a public manner.* This is better than to have things go to pieces; but the influence of both the extremes and the reproofs are terrible on the cause, and brings upon Mrs. White a threefold burden. Here is the difficulty: *What she may say to urge the tardy, is taken by the prompt to urge them over the mark. And what she may say to caution the prompt, zealous, incautious ones, is taken by the tardy as an excuse to remain too far behind*" (RH, Mar. 17, 1868; italics supplied).

A case that illustrates the difficulty James White spoke to in his 1868 article relates to Ellen White's counsel on "speedy preparation for the work." On March 21, 1895, she penned an extensive and hard-hitting article by that title (see FE 334-367) aimed at some of the improper emphases and attitudes in evidence at Battle Creek College. The article contained some strong statements in it because she was combating deeply entrenched misconceptions and wanted to speak "loudly" enough to be heard. She believed some of the teachers sought to keep the students in school too long and were giving them more depth than needed in certain lines of study. "If we had a thousand years before us," she penned in seeking to make her point, "such a depth of knowledge would be uncalled for" *(ibid.* 334).

But some of her zealous reform readers took her words to mean that they should go to the opposite extreme. As a result, on April 22 she wrote two balancing testimonies in an attempt to pull the reformers back toward the center *(ibid.* 368-380). "No movement," she wrote, "should be made to lower the standard of education in our school at Battle Creek. The students should tax the mental powers; every faculty should reach the highest possible development. . . .

"I hope that no one will receive the impression from any words I have written, that the standard of the school is to be in any way lowered. There should be most diligent and thorough education in our school" *(ibid.* 373).

What Ellen White was really trying to tell the administration and faculty of the school was that they needed to come to grips with the foundational principles of what made Christian education Christian within the context of quality education. But, as usual, the extremists collected all the most forceful quotations, while those desiring the status quo undoubtedly focused their attention on the conservative statements she gave to correct those tending toward fanaticism. Both sides may have missed Ellen White's intent because of the weaknesses of human communication.

Another illustration of Ellen White's use of extreme language to get someone's attention had to do with Dr. John Harvey Kellogg, director of the Battle Creek Sanitarium. In 1901 she noted to a group of church leaders that she had been worried about Kellogg's spiritual state for some time. "I have written some very straight things to him," she told her audience, "and it may be, Dr. Kellogg (if he is here), that I have written too strong; for I felt as though I must get hold of you and hold you by the power of all the might I had" (MS 43a, 1901).

As we read Ellen White's writings we need to keep constantly before us the difficulty she faced in basic communication. Beyond the difficulty of varying personalities, but related to it, was the problem of the imprecision of the meaning of words and the fact that different people with different experiences interpret the same words differently.

"Human minds vary," Mrs. White penned in relation to Bible reading. *"The minds of different education and thought receive different impressions of the same words,* and it is difficult for one mind to give to one of a different temperament, education, and habits of thought by language exactly the same idea as that which is clear and distinct in his own mind. . . .

"The writers of the Bible had to express their ideas in human language. . . .

"The Bible is not given to us in grand superhuman language. . . . *The Bible must be given in the language of men. Everything that is human is imperfect. Different meanings are expressed by the same word;* there is not one word for each distinct idea. The Bible was given for practical purposes.

"The stamps of minds are different. All do not understand expressions and statements alike. Some understand the statements of the Scriptures to suit their own particular minds and cases. Prepossessions, prejudices, and passions have a strong influence to darken the understanding and confuse the mind even in reading the words of Holy Writ" (1SM 19, 20; italics supplied).

What Ellen White said about the problems of meanings and words in regard to the Bible also holds true for her own writings. Communication in a broken world is never easy, not even for God's prophets. On the other hand, we don't need perfect knowledge in order to be saved. As Ellen White repeatedly notes, the Bible (and her writings) was given for "practical purposes." Human language, in spite of its weaknesses, is capable of communicating the essence of the plan of salvation and Christian responsibility to those who honestly desire to know God's truth *(ibid.)*.

The communication problems stemming from different mind-sets, personality types, and backgrounds even enter into the reasons for having more than one account of the life of Christ in the New Testament. The following statement helps us appreciate the challenges God faced in communicating with intelligent beings on a sinful planet.

"Why do we need," wrote Ellen White, "a Matthew, a Mark, a Luke, a John, a Paul, and all the writers who have borne testimony in regard to the life and ministry of the Saviour? Why could not one of the disciples have written a complete record and thus have given us a connected account of Christ's earthly life? Why does one writer bring in points that another does not mention? Why, if these points are essential, did not all these writers mention them? It is because the minds of men differ. Not all comprehend things in exactly the same way" (CT 432).

We need to keep the basic problems of communication that we have examined in this chapter in mind as we read the writings of Ellen White. At the very least, such facts ought to make us cautious in our reading so that we don't overly emphasize this or that particular idea that might come to our attention as we study God's counsel to His church. We will want to make sure that we have read widely what Ellen White has presented on a topic and study those statements that may seem extreme in the light of those that might moderate or balance them. All such study, of course, should take place with the historical and literary context of each statement in mind. It is to those four concerns that we turn to in chapters 10 through 13.

Chapter Ten

Study All Available Information on a Topic

e have come to a most important subject for a healthy reading of Ellen White's writings. A familiar poem illustrates my point.

It was six men of Indostan
    To learning much inclined,
Who went to see the elephant
    (Though all of them were blind),
That each by observation
    Might satisfy his mind.

The first approached the elephant,
    And happening to fall
Against his broad and sturdy side,
    At once began to bawl,
"Why, bless me! but the elephant
    Is very like a wall!"

The second, feeling of the tusk,
    Cried: "Ho, what have we here
So very round and smooth and sharp?

To me 'tis mighty clear
This wonder of an elephant
Is very like a spear!"

The third approached the animal,
And, happening to take
The squirming trunk within his hands,
Thus boldly up and spake:
"I see," quoth he, "the elephant
Is very like a snake!"

The fourth reached out his eager hand,
And felt about the knee;
"What most this wondrous beast is like
Is mighty plain," quoth he;
" 'Tis clear enough, the elephant
Is very like a tree!"

The fifth, who chanced to touch the ear,
Said: "E'en the blindest man
Can tell what this resembles most.
Deny the fact who can,
This marvel of an elephant
Is very like a fan!"

The sixth no sooner had begun
About the beast to grope,
Than, seizing on the swinging tail
That fell within his scope,
"I see," quoth he, "the elephant
Is very like a rope!"

And so these men of Indostan
Disputed loud and long,
Each in his own opinion
Exceeding stiff and strong,

> Though each was partly in the right,
> And all were in the wrong!
> —John Godfrey Saxe

The poem illustrates a difficulty that it is all too easy to fall into when reading Ellen White's massive literary output—the danger of not examining the full spectrum of available information from her pen on a topic. Arthur White pinpointed the issue when he wrote that "many have erred in interpreting the meaning of the testimonies by taking isolated statements or statements out of their context as a basis for belief. Some do this even though there are other passages, which, if carefully considered, would show the position taken on the basis of the isolated statement to be untenable. . . .

"It is not difficult to find individual sentences or paragraphs in either the Bible or the Ellen G. White writings, which may be used to support one's own ideas rather than to set forth the thought of the author" (*Ellen G. White: Messenger to the Remnant,* p. 88).

That quotation reminds me of an experience I had as a young pastor in the San Francisco Bay Area. I had made friends with a zealous and sincere group of Adventists who wanted to follow the Bible and the writings of Ellen White with all their hearts. If Mrs. White said it, they did it. There was no discussing an issue once they had her words on the topic. They were going to be faithful to what they referred to as the "straight testimony."

I still remember the first time I attended a small church that my friends had organized. The thing that caught me off guard was that they knelt for *every* prayer. Thus the congregation sang a song, then knelt for the invocation; heard the special music and took the offering, then knelt for the offering prayer; sang a song, then knelt for the pastoral prayer; heard the speaker introduced, then knelt for prayer at the beginning of the sermon; listened to the sermon and sang the closing song, then knelt for the benediction.

As the guest speaker for the day, I followed the congregation and its leaders in the repeated kneeling throughout the service. But being somewhat perplexed at what I had experienced, soon after the service I asked the group's founder (who had the reputation of being an expert on Mrs. White's writings) about the reason for kneeling for every prayer.

In response, he read excerpts to me from the second volume of *Selected Messages,* pages 311-316: "I have received letters questioning me in regard to the proper attitude to be taken by a person offering prayer to the Sovereign of the universe. Where have our brethren obtained the idea that they should stand upon their feet when praying to God?" (p. 311). My friend pointed out that Ellen White went on to say that "the proper position *always*" for prayer is on our knees *(ibid.;* italics supplied). "Both in public and private worship it is our duty to bow down upon our knees before God when we offer our petitions to Him. This act shows our dependence upon God" *(ibid.* 312).

I assured my friend that I believed in reverence and kneeling in prayer, but I also told him that his interpretation of Ellen White's passage seemed strained to me and out of harmony with the general tenor of her writings.

He flatly disagreed, since he had her words and that was enough. If she said *"always,"* they would *always* kneel in prayer. There was no need to talk the matter over or to read more on the topic. After all, when one has "the truth" on a topic, all that remains is to put it into practice. And he did. I even remember kneeling for grace before meals at his home.

I wasn't at all convinced that my friend had "the truth" on the topic, even though I was absolutely sure that he had a few "quotations" from Ellen White to substantiate his practice. But *there is a difference between a handful of quotations and the truth.*

How, you may be thinking, *can I be so sure of my point?* It's not all that complicated. I merely kept on reading on the topic of the correct position in prayer. In this case I didn't have to read very far. On the last page of the section "The Attitude in Prayer" in *Selected Messages* that my friend had quoted from, I read that "it is *not always necessary to bow upon your knees* in order to pray. Cultivate the habit of talking with the Saviour when you are alone, when you are walking, and when you are busy with your daily labor" *(ibid.* 316; italics supplied).

That is one of three quotations that the White Estate (the compilers of *Selected Messages)* deliberately put at the end of the section on reverence in prayer to steer people away from the kind of one-sidedness that had captured my friend—a one-sidedness that can easily lead to fanaticism.

When I pointed out the balancing statements on kneeling for prayer and asked why he insisted on reading Ellen White only as meaning *always* when she also said "not always," he quickly argued that the not-always statements reflected on the general public and not God's special end-time people.

That, I mused to myself, is the nice thing about "having the truth" in the way my friend had it. Once you had it you could conveniently forget the other half of what Ellen White (or the Bible) had to say on a topic and push ahead on your own narrow course.

Thus my friend was absolutely convinced that God's faithful last-day remnant should lead the way in restoring prayer to what it should be. He was God's man for the hour to guide God's people back to the truth on the issue of *always* kneeling in prayer.

While I agreed with him that reverence needed to increase in many churches, I couldn't accept what seemed to be a one-sided conclusion. What should I do? The answer was simple. I had two tasks ahead of me. The first was to continue reading on the topic. The second was to write the Ellen G. White Estate at General Conference headquarters to see if they had any further information on the topic. Both strategies paid off in increasing my understanding. And, I hasten to add, both strategies are open to every person who has a question regarding Ellen White and her writings. Don't be afraid to contact the White Estate with your queries. They can supply you with some excellent information on Ellen White's overall position on a topic as well as where to start reading to round out your understanding.

Before long I arrived at a fuller picture of the subject of the position of prayer for God's people. Not only did I discover the Bible approved prayers in which the position was something other than kneeling (see, for example, Mark 11:25; Ex. 34:8), but I found Ellen

White confiding to a friend that she sometimes prayed "for hours while lying in my bed" (letter 258, 1903). That hardly sounds like "always" kneeling "both in public and in private worship."

Beyond that, I eventually came across a letter by a longtime associate of Ellen White in which he stated: "I have been present repeatedly at camp meetings and General Conference sessions in which Sister White herself has offered prayer with the congregation standing, and she herself standing" (D. E. Robinson to W. E. Daylish, Mar. 4, 1934).

References to some of those standing prayers appear in Mrs. White's own published writings. For example, at the 1909 General Conference session Ellen White, after speaking, brought the meeting to a close by asking the congregation to rise to their "feet" in dedication. She then, while they were still standing, led them in a prayer to the "Lord God of Israel" (1SM 152). You will find other such occasions in *Selected Messages,* book 3, pages 266-270.

When we read the full range of counsel that Ellen White has on a topic, the picture is often quite different than when we are dealing with only a part of her material or with isolated quotations. After reading all I could easily find on the topic of the proper position in prayer, I concluded that my friend was advocating an extreme position that lacked the balance of Ellen White's full spectrum of counsel on the topic.

In retrospect, having examined all available counsel on the issue of kneeling for prayer, I've come to believe that Ellen White was concerned with a lack of reverence in the Adventist Church reflected in some cases by congregations not kneeling for prayer during the main prayer of the day. The position for that prayer was "always," where possible, to be kneeling. But nowhere in her writings do we find her advocating kneeling for benedictions, invocations, grace before meals, and so on. Her general teaching is that it is "not always" necessary to kneel for every prayer. Such appears to be not only her teaching but also her practice.

Many times in her long ministry Ellen White had to deal with those who took only part of her counsel. "When it suits your purpose," she told the delegates of the 1891 General Conference session, "you treat the Testimonies as if you believed them, quoting from them to strengthen any statement you wish to have prevail. But how is it when light is given to correct your errors? Do you then accept the light? When the Testimonies speak contrary to your ideas, you treat them very lightly" (1SM 43). It is important to listen to all the counsel.

Along this line we find two approaches to the Ellen G. White writings. One assembles all pertinent E. G. White material on the subject. The other selects from Mrs. White only those sentences, paragraphs, or more extensive materials that can be employed to support a particular emphasis. The only faithful approach is the first. One important step in being true to Ellen White's intent is to read widely in the available counsel on a topic.

But not only must we base our conclusion on the entire spectrum of her thought on a topic; our conclusion must harmonize with the overall tenor of the body of her writings. Not only bias, but also unsound premises, faulty reasoning, or other misuses of her material, can lead to false conclusions.

Chapter Eleven

Avoid Extreme Interpretations

Stephen N. Haskell, a prominent Seventh-day Adventist minister during the last quarter of the nineteenth century, returned to the United States after a tour of duty in Australia to discover many "queer doctrines preached by some of the leading ministers of the rising generation." As might be expected, they quoted from the *Testimonies* and the Bible to prove their points, so much so that "one not grounded in the principles of the [Adventist] message would be carried away with them."

"Some of the strangest doctrines I have heard," reported Haskell, "is the Seal of God cannot be placed on any person of gray hairs, or any deformed person, for in the closing work we would reach a state of perfection both physically and spiritually, where we would be healed from all physical deformity and then could not die, etc." Some expected to get a new set of teeth in this life, and "one woman said how convincing it would be to her friends to see her return home with her hairs all restored and believed it would be soon" (S. N. Haskell to E. G. White, Oct. 3, 1899). Seven weeks later Haskell had to deal with a related extremist teaching that on the basis of the Ten Commandments it was wrong to kill poisonous snakes or harmful insects (see S. N. Haskell to E. G. White, Nov. 23, 1899).

The history of the Christian church is laced with those who would place the most extreme interpretations on God's counsels and then define their fanaticism as "faithfulness." Unfortunately, the same has been true of some in the Adventist branch of the Christian tree. A leaning toward extremism seems to be a constituent part of fallen human nature. God has sought to correct that tendency through His prophets.

One of the major themes of this chapter is that even though balance typified Ellen White's writings, it does not always characterize those who read them. A case in point is Ellen White's counsel to a physician who had taken "extreme views of health reform" after reading her writings. "Health reform," she wrote to Dr. D. H. Kress, "becomes *health deform,* a health destroyer, when it is carried to extremes" (CD 202; italics supplied).

James White raises the same issue. "While Satan tempts the many to be too slow, he always tempts" others "to be too fast. Mrs. White's labors are made very hard, and sometimes perplexing, by reason of the course of extremists, who think the only safe position is to take the extreme view of every expression she has written or spoken upon points where different views may be taken.

"These persons will often hang upon their interpretation of an expression, and push matters at all hazards, and utterly disregard what she has said of the danger of extremes. *We suggest that these loosen their hold of some of her strong expressions designed to move the tardy, and for awhile suspend their whole weight upon some of the many cautions she has given for the benefit of extremists.* In doing this, they will be more safe themselves, and will get out of her way, that she may speak freely to those who need urging to duty. Now they stand between her and the people, and paralyze her testimony, and are the cause of divisions" (RH, Mar. 17, 1868; italics supplied).

Ellen White had to deal with extremists throughout her ministry. In 1894 she pointed out that "there is a class of people who are always ready to go off on some tangent, who want to catch up something strange and wonderful and new; but God would have all move calmly, considerately, choosing our words in harmony with the solid truth for this time, which requires to be presented to the mind as free from that which is emotional as possible, while still bearing the intensity and solemnity that it is proper it should bear. We must guard against creating extremes, guard against encouraging those who would either be in the fire or in the water" (TM 227, 228).

Nearly four decades earlier Mrs. White had written that she "saw that many have taken advantage of what God has shown in regard to the sins and wrongs of others. They have taken the extreme meaning of what has been shown in vision, and then have pressed it until it has had a tendency to weaken the faith of many in what God has shown" (1T 166).

The tragic thing is that some in urging extreme statements in certain areas such as health reform have pushed their understandings on what is central and sinful to the point that if they are correct, then Ellen White must be a false prophet, since their extreme interpretations make her not only go beyond the Bible, but even contradict it. For example, whereas Paul said that "the kingdom of God is not food and drink but righteousness and peace and joy in the Holy Spirit" (Rom. 14:17, RSV), some of Ellen White's interpreters would push that aspect of her teaching to center stage.

Mrs. White herself was quite in harmony with Paul. When individuals in her day sought to put health reform at the center because she had said that it was as closely connected with God's last message to the world "as are the arm and hand with the human body" (1T 486), she cautioned them that "the health reform is closely connected with the work of the third message [of Revelation 14], yet it is not the message. Our preachers should teach the health reform, yet they should not make this the leading theme in the place of the message." She told her readers that health reform had an important "preparatory" role to play in final events (1T 559). That idea fits in nicely with a remark she made in another connection. "The last rays of merciful light, the last message of mercy to be given to the world, is a revelation of His [God's] character of love. The children of God are to manifest His glory. In their own life and character they are to reveal what the grace of God has done for them" (COL 415, 416).

Health reform is "preparatory" in the final work in the sense that we are less than adequate lovers of others and even of God when our stomachs are sour, our heads ache, and so on. God wants to demonstrate in His children that transforming grace can indeed make selfish people into loving and caring ones. While health reform is one means to such an end, it is not an end in itself. To put it or certain other such topics at the center of our spiritual lives is to miss not only their purpose but also how they fit into God's total message through Ellen White.

Part of our task in reading Ellen White is to avoid extreme interpretations and to understand her message in its proper balance. That in turn means that we need to read the counsel from both ends of the spectrum on a given topic.

A case in point is her strong words about playing games. "In plunging into amusements, match games, pugilistic performances," she wrote, the students at Battle Creek College "declared to the world that Christ was not their leader in any of these things. All this called forth the warning from God." A powerful statement, it and others like it have led many to the conclusion that God frowns on *all* games and ball playing. But here, as on all extreme interpretations, one should use caution. After all, the *very next* sentence reads: "Now that which burdens me is the danger of going into extremes on the other side" (FE 378).

As the following statements demonstrate, Ellen White did not hold for either extreme on the topic of ball playing and games. Speaking of parents and teachers, she wrote: "If they would gather the children close to them, and show that they love them, and would manifest an interest in all their efforts, and even in their sports, sometimes even being a child among children, they would make the children very happy, and would gain their love and win their confidence" (*ibid.* 18).

As we noted in chapter 10, it is important to read the full spectrum of what Ellen White wrote on a topic before arriving at conclusions. That means taking into consideration what appear to be conflicting statements that not only balance each other but may at times even appear to contradict each other. Of course, as we shall see in the next two chapters, the historical and literary contexts generally hold the reason for Ellen White's extreme statements. When we understand the reason she said something a certain way, we can see how what appears to be contradictory bits of advice often balance each other out. With those understandings in place we will be ready to examine the underlying principles of the particular topic we are studying. We will return to the importance of underlying principles in chapter 16. Meanwhile, let's read a third statement on ball playing and games.

"I do not," penned Ellen White, "condemn the simple exercise of playing ball; but this, even in its simplicity, may be overdone" (AH 499). The problem as she set it forth in this moderating statement is not in the doing, but in the overdoing and misdoing of ball playing in terms of both time and the complexity of arrangements that leads to difficulties in interpersonal relationships. She went on to note that all too often ball games resulted in inordinate expenditures of money, self-glorification, a love and enthusiasm for games more than Christ, and a "burning passion" for supremacy. In addition, she noted, the way people often play games does not strengthen the intellect or character, distracts minds from studies, and tends to make their participants lovers of pleasure more than of God (*ibid.* 499, 500).

When we read the balancing and mediating passages on a topic, rather than merely those polar ones that reinforce our own biases, we come closer to Ellen White's true perspective. The moral of the story is clear. In order to avoid extreme interpretations, we need not only to read widely regarding what Mrs. White said on a topic, but we need also to come to grips with those statements that balance each other out at each end of the spectrum on a given subject.

Another helpful illustration of the necessity of reading the balancing counsel on a topic has to do with the use of eggs. You will recall from chapter 1 that Ellen White wrote that "eggs should not be placed upon your table. They are an injury to your children" (2T 400). She made that statement to a family whose children were struggling with sensuality. The counsel had to do with their specific situation.

But many understood it as an absolute prohibition. As a result, Dr. D. H. Kress, a conscientious medical doctor serving as a missionary in Australia, totally banned eggs from his table, along with dairy products and many other articles of food. His deprived diet eventually led to deficiencies that seriously threatened his health.

As a result, Ellen White wrote to him in May 1901, urging that he should "not go to extremes in regard to the health reform. . . . Get eggs of healthy fowls. Use these eggs cooked or raw. Drop them uncooked into the best unfermented wine you can find. This will supply that which is necessary to your system. Do not for a moment suppose that it will not be right to do this. . . . I say that milk and eggs should be included in your diet. . . . You are in danger of taking too radical a view of health reform, and of prescribing for yourself a diet that will not sustain you. . . . Eggs contain properties which are remedial agencies in counteracting poisons. And while warnings have been given against the use of these articles of diet in families where the children were addicted to, yes, steeped in, habits of self-abuse; yet we should not consider it a denial of principle to use eggs of hens which are well cared for" (letter 37, 1901; much of this letter appears in CD 202-206).

Note the contextual factors in this counsel, and that she directed it toward a specific problem. Also observe the principles Ellen White is setting forth. For example, it is best to eat eggs from "hens which are well cared for and suitably fed." We will return to the topics of contextualization and the importance of principles in future chapters. But first, let's spend a bit more time with Dr. Kress.

Kress replied to Ellen White the next month. "I can see," he wrote, "that the strong view I held with reference to the milk and egg question placed me in danger of going to extremes, and I feel very thankful that the Lord has corrected me. . . . Now with reference to myself as far as I know I am following out carefully all the instruction that God has sent me through you. I am using both the eggs and the milk, and I am able to do so without a prick of conscience now. Before this I could not do it without feeling condemned, and I really believe there is hope for me being restored to health, else the Lord would not have sent this message" (D. H. Kress to E. G. White, June 28, 1901).

Forty-three years later Kress reflected back on his experience. "Some honest souls have taken an extreme position in regard to some of the statements made by Sister White regarding the use of animal food products, especially milk and eggs." Speaking to his own extremes, he said, "I ran down in health almost to the point of death. . . . Sister White saw me in vision and wrote me several letters, pointing out the cause of my condition, and urging me to make a change in my dietetic habits. . . . After receiving this message, I at once began making reforms by using eggs as directed, and milk, and with God's blessing I made a good recovery. . . . This was over forty years ago. I have now about reached my eighty-second year of life, and am still able to spend three hours daily in my office at the Sanitarium. For the health so graciously granted me, I am indebted to the messages that came to me at a time when a recovery seemed hopeless from a human standpoint. I still follow out the instruction by using milk and eggs" (D. H. Kress, unpublished MS, Jan. 6, 1944).

Dr. Kress was apparently thankful to the end of his days that Ellen White had guided him away from making extreme interpretations of her writings.

Chapter Twelve

Take Time and Place
Into Consideration

It was my first day as principal of a metropolitan junior academy. It was also the era of the miniskirt. I will never forget my first phone call. "Brother Knight," exclaimed the woman's voice on the other end of the line, "we are so thankful that we at last have a principal who will enforce standards!"

I soon discovered that she believed her daughter's skirts were too short. My first thought was to ask her why she didn't do something about it, but the Lord helped me hold my tongue as she went on and on and on and on regarding short skirts. While managing to control my tongue on this occasion, I found it next to impossible to keep my mind from wandering. I heard her telling me that in some academies they had a rule that skirts could be no shorter than two inches above the knee. At that point the distasteful mental image arose of me touring the campus with a ruler in one hand as I grabbed my high school girls by the knee for their daily measurement.

As the parent kept talking, my mind continued to wander. I visualized a girl at five feet eleven inches. Two inches above the knee might be quite long. But I had a chubby tenth grader who was four feet nine inches. Two inches above her knee would be halfway to her waist. My mind then went to a suggestion that

Ellen White had made in the 1860s that women should shorten their skirts eight or nine inches. Now, there was an interesting thought. To shorten some of the skirts that I had seen in the late 1960s and early 1970s by eight or nine inches would have put the bottom of the hemline somewhere above the top of the waistband.

By this time you may be wondering where I am going with this illustration. My point is really quite simple. We need to take the time and place of Ellen White's various counsels into consideration. She did not write them in a vacuum. Most of them met problems faced by specific individuals or groups in quite specific historic contexts.

Now, it doesn't take a great deal of insight to know that to cite Ellen White on shortening skirts by eight or nine inches was quite inappropriate in the age of the miniskirt. That is obvious. But, and this is an important point, for many other statements it is not nearly so clear as to whether they apply exactly to a specific individual in another time and place. It takes study into the original counsel in its historic context to make such determinations. Several of the chapters that follow will help us in that endeavor.

Meanwhile, why did Mrs. White suggest that women should shorten their skirts? Because in her day skirts dragged on the ground. In the process they picked up the filth of a horse-and-buggy culture among other things. Such skirts also had other problems that Ellen White and contemporary reformers of her day repeatedly pointed out. Thus she could write that "one of fashion's wasteful and mischievous devices is the skirt that sweeps the ground. Uncleanly, uncomfortable, inconvenient, unhealthful— all this and more is true of the trailing skirt" (MH 291).

But what was true of her day is generally not true of ours. Of course, one can think of some traditional cultures that still mirror the conditions of the nineteenth century. In those cultures the counsel fits without adaptation. But we must adapt it for most cultures today.

Part of the needed adaptation is reflected in *The Ministry of Healing* quotation we read above. If the problem with trailing skirts was that they were unclean, uncomfortable, inconvenient, and unhealthful, then it seems safe to assume that some of the principles of correct dress in this case would be that it is clean, comfortable, convenient, and healthful. Such principles are universal, even though the idea of shortening one's skirt has roots in time and place. Further reading in the Bible and Ellen White furnishes other principles of dress that we can apply to our day. Modesty, for example, comes to mind.

You may be wondering what my school did to care for its miniskirt problem. We certainly didn't unthinkingly use Ellen White's admonition to shorten skirts. Nor did I run around with a ruler in my hand measuring the distance between knees and hemlines. To the contrary, we took the principles set forth on the topic in the Bible and Ellen White and applied them to our time and place. When we brought our young ladies together, we told them that we expected their dress to be clean, neat, modest, and so on.

But the extracting of principles from Ellen White's writings is not the topic of this chapter. We will return to that subject in chapter 16.

Another helpful illustration of the need to take time and place into consideration is her counsel on courtship. In 1897 Mrs. White wrote of the students of the Avondale school in Australia that "we would not, could not, allow any courting or forming attachments at the school, girls with young men and young men with girls" (letter 193, 1897). The same year she penned that "we have labored hard [at Avondale] to keep in check everything in the school like favoritism, attachments, and courting. We have told the students that we would not allow the first thread of this to be interwoven with their schoolwork. On this point we are as firm as a rock" (letter 145, 1897).

Avondale published the statement in its school announcements. There is no doubt that C. W. Irwin, principal of Avondale from 1903 to 1908, was "firm as a rock" on the subject of courting. In 1913 Irwin, then serving as president of Pacific Union College in California, was asked to read the manuscript for Ellen White's forthcoming *Counsels to Parents, Teachers, and Students.*

Irwin was shocked to find the strict courtship statement he had been enforcing missing from the new book. In its place he found a much milder statement with the following qualifications: "In all our dealings with students, age and character must be taken into account. We cannot treat the young and the old just alike. There are circumstances under which men and women of sound experience and good standing may be granted some privileges not given to the younger students. The age, the conditions, and the turn of mind must be taken into consideration. We must be wisely considerate in all our work. But we must not lessen our firmness and vigilance in dealing with students of all ages, nor our strictness in forbidding the unprofitable and unwise association of young and immature students" (CT 101).

The change in tone from her previous counsel on the topic troubled Irwin. He wrote to W. C. White claiming that the instruction was "something entirely new" and that he was "at a loss to know how to make it agree with matter which Sister White has written on other occasions, all of which . . . has been perfectly consistent with itself" (C. W. Irwin to W. C. White, Feb. 12, 1913).

What Irwin had not taken into account was the difference in circumstances in which Ellen White had given the seemingly divergent counsel. Her counsel to the Avondale school in 1897 focused on a situation in which nearly half the students were under 16 years of age. But in 1913 the majority of students in the denomination's colleges were older, more experienced, and more mature. Ellen White in providing *general counsel* for the church at large took the changed circumstances into account.

W. C. White's reply to Irwin is insightful concerning the importance of time and place in Ellen White's counsel. "One of the most perplexing problems we have to deal with in preparing Mother's writings for publication," her son penned, "is in just such matters as this, where the conditions of a family, or a church, or an institution are presented to her, and warnings and instruction are given regarding these conditions. In such cases Mother writes clearly and forcefully, and without qualification regarding the situation presented to her, and it is a great blessing to us that we have this instruction for our study in dealing with similar conditions elsewhere. But *when we take what she has written, and publish it without any description, or particular reference to the conditions existing when and where the testimony was given, there is always the possibility of the instruction being used as applying to places and conditions that are very different.*

"Very much perplexity has been brought into our work in this way, by the use of what Mother has written on the subject of diet, and on the use of drugs, and on other subjects that you will think of without my enumerating them; and when the time has come for instruction to be given to some individual, or family, or church, *which presented the right course to be taken, under conditions which were different from those contemplated in former writings, the exception made, or the different course advised in view of the different conditions, has often come as a surprise to those who felt that the instruction they have been studying, was of universal application*" (W. C. White to C. W. Irwin, Feb. 18, 1913; italics supplied).

It can't be too heavily emphasized that time and place are crucial factors for our understanding as we read Ellen White's writings. Along this line, Mrs. White wrote that *"regarding the testimonies,* nothing is ignored; nothing is cast aside; but *time and place must be considered.* Nothing must be done untimely. Some matters must be withheld because some persons would make an improper use of the light given" (1SM 57; italics supplied). One way to use her writings improperly is to ignore the implications of time and place and thus seek to apply the letter of each and every counsel universally.

The role of time and place is important in interpreting the Bible also. Thus, for example, most Christians do not take off their shoes when they enter a church, even though God Himself commanded Moses to do so in meeting with Him (Ex. 3:5).

In Ellen White's writings such counsels as those urging schools to teach girls "to harness and drive a horse" so "they would be better fitted to meet the emergencies of life" (Ed 216, 217); warning both young and old in 1894 to avoid the "bewitching influence" of the "bicycle craze" (8T 51, 52); and counseling an administrator in 1902 not to buy an automobile to transport patients from the railroad station to the sanitarium because it was a needless expense and would prove to be "a temptation to others to do the same thing" (letter 158, 1902) are clearly conditioned by time and place. Other statements that may also be conditioned by time and place are not so obvious (especially in those areas we tend to feel strongly about), but we need to keep our eyes and mind open to the possibility.

Another aspect of the time and place issue in Ellen White's writing is that for many of her counsels the historical context is quite personal, since she wrote to an individual in his or her specific setting. Always remember that behind every counsel lies a specific situation with its own peculiarities and/or an individual with his or her personal possibilities and problems. Their situation may or may not be parallel to ours. Thus the counsel may or may not be applicable to us in a given circumstance.

One illustration of that point is the case of M. L. Andreasen, a leading Adventist theologian of the 1930s and 1940s. Andreasen's experience illustrates the situation of a person who readily admits that he had backed himself into an extreme corner on health reform and then compounded his problem by applying a statement on overeating to himself. Let Andreasen tell his story.

"I passed through the health reform period in the early part of the century. *We took health reform seriously and in its extreme meaning.* I lived practically on granola and water only. . . . I used neither milk, butter, nor eggs [for a period of years]. My older daughter was ten years old when she first tasted butter. We used no meat, of course, nor milk, butter, or eggs, and almost no salt and sugar. We did not have much left but granola. I canvassed on granola. It never occurred to me to accept an invitation to a meal. I carried my granola with me in a sack. I sold granola also. That was part of health reform. I ate my granola and drank water three times a day. Then my attention was called to the fact that two times were better and so I ate granola twice a day. . . .

"But I got tired of granola alone after a while. I wondered if it would be all right to eat raisins with it; and so I bought some raisins with a little trepidation and anxiety. Now it was granola and raisins, but my conscience smote me, so I gave up the raisins. Then I bought a pineapple and ate all of it, with the result that my mouth became sore. I took that to be punishment for eating pineapples. So I went back to granola again. Then I read somewhere in Sister White's writings that people eat altogether too much. I applied that to my two meals of granola a day. *That statement in itself is true, but not under those conditions.* I cut down on my granola and henceforth lived mostly on granola and a few simple vegetables and peanuts, not for a day or a month or a year, but for ten years.

"We were serious and honest in doing this, and thought we had testimony for it—not testimony in its broad application but only in that narrow sense which some apply today. The principles in the *Testimonies* in regard to health reform are true and applicable now as they were then, under like conditions. Let no one set aside the *Testimonies*. They are given of God. *But let all beware lest they apply {Ellen White's counsels} to conditions other than those under which they were given*" (M. L. Andreasen, unpublished MS, Nov. 30, 1948; italics supplied).

Andreasen was obviously sincere, but he was just as obviously wrong in applying Ellen White's statement about overeating to himself. As the years passed he grew in his understanding of how to read Ellen White's writings. Not only did he back away from his extreme diet, but he came to recognize specific personal situations behind many of her statements that did not apply to himself or to his times. He also saw that even general contexts changed. As a result, he retreated from many of his extremes on health reform as he came to realize that pasteurization and refrigeration had "changed conditions" for some articles of food he had earlier deemed unhealthy. Thus he increasingly understood that time and place are of crucial importance in understanding Ellen White's counsel *(ibid.)*.

Unfortunately, the church has not published a great deal on the historical background of Ellen White's writings. My own *Myths in Adventism: An Interpretive Study of Ellen White, Education, and Related Issues* (Review and Herald, 1985) has done some of that background work. Dores E. Robinson's *The Story of Our Health Message* (Southern Publishing Assn., 1955) also makes a contribution in this line. Paul Gordon is doing additional historical work in what he has tentatively titled "Testimony Backgrounds." On a more general level, Gary Land's *The World of Ellen G. White* (Review and Herald, 1987) and Otto L. Bettmann's *The Good Old Days—They Were Terrible!* (Random House, 1974) are quite helpful. Bettmann's book is especially fascinating, since it sets forth the conditions of Ellen White's world pictorially.

Chapter Thirteen

Study Each Statement in Its Literary Context

In chapter 12 we noted that it is important to understand Ellen White's counsel in its original historical context. In this chapter we will examine the importance of reading her statements in their literary framework.

People have too often based their understandings of Mrs. White's teachings upon a fragment of a paragraph or upon an isolated statement entirely removed from its setting. Thus she writes that "many study the Scriptures for the purpose of proving their own ideas to be correct. They change the meaning of God's Word to suit their own opinions. And thus they do also with the testimonies that He sends. They quote half a sentence, leaving out the other half, which, if quoted, would show their reasoning to be false. God has a controversy with those who wrest the Scriptures, making them conform to their preconceived ideas" (3SM 82). Again she comments about those who by "separating . . . statements from their connection, and placing them beside human reasonings, make it appear that my writings uphold that which they condemn" (letter 208, 1906).

Ellen White was repeatedly upset with those who pick out "a sentence here and there, taking it from its proper connection, and applying it according to their idea." Such "poor souls," she noted, became "bewildered, when could they read in order all that has been given, they would see the true application, and would not become confused" (1SM 44). On another occasion she observed that "extracts" from her writings "may give a different impression than that which they would were they read in their original connection" (*ibid.* 58).

W. C. White often had to deal with the problem of people using material out of its literary context. In 1904 he noted that "much misunderstanding has come from the misuse of isolated passages in the Testimonies, in cases where, if the whole Testimony or the whole paragraph had been read, an impression would have been made upon minds that was altogether different from the impression made by the use of selected sentences" (W. C. White to W. S. Sadler, Jan. 20, 1904).

He made one of his more revealing statements on the topic in 1911. On that occasion he wrote to a Brother Brisbin, who had compiled a booklet on health reform from Ellen White's writings. Brisbin had written in May of that year wondering why he had received no reply to an earlier letter regarding his compilation and raising "the question as to whether the Testimonies to the church forbid the making of compilations from the writings of Sister White."

White replied in October that one reason for his tardy reply had been his mother's "unwillingness to read the matter that you have collected from her writings" for the health reform booklet.

As to her attitude toward selecting abstracts from her writings to make a private compilation, W. C. White had the following to say: "Sister White maintains that to be properly understood, her writings should be read in their connection. She says that she was not commissioned of God to write proverbs. Moreover she feels that it is an injury to the cause of truth for men to select from her writings short passages here and there, presenting her strongest statements on one phase of a subject, while leaving out other qualifying passages, and such presentation of other phases of the subject as are essential to a well-balanced and comprehensive view of her teachings.

"She says: If those advocating health reform will take my books where all phases of these subjects are presented, or if they will study my articles as a whole, they will get precious truths. . . . But for them to take a sentence here, and a paragraph there, and a few lines somewhere else, and group them together according to their fancy or judgment, they may sadly misrepresent my teachings and give the people distorted views of Health Reform, or of whatever subject they are handling" (W. C. White to W. L. Brisbin, Oct. 10, 1911).

A case in point regarding taking sentences out of context has to do with eating fruits and vegetables at the same meal. "It is not well to eat fruit and vegetables at the same meal," we read in *The Ministry of Healing* (p. 299). Some, taking that statement out of its literary context, have made it into a rule applicable to all. But they need to read on. The very next words declare: *"If the digestion is feeble,* the use of both will often cause distress and inability to put forth mental effort." For such people, she concludes, "it is better to have the fruit at one meal and the vegetables at another" (*ibid.* 299, 300; italics supplied).

On another occasion she counseled that "if we would preserve the best health, we should avoid eating vegetables and fruit at the same meal. *If the stomach is feeble,* there will be distress, the brain will be confused, and unable to put forth mental effort. Have fruit at one meal and vegetables at the next" (CD 395; italics supplied).

Arthur White, late director of the Ellen G. White Estate, in commenting on these quotations, notes that "inasmuch as Ellen White mentions impaired digestion as a factor in this matter, it would seem that it would be carrying matters too far to make this a hard and fast rule which would apply in every degree. In fact, we observe that she states that in the field of desserts, fruit if it can be obtained is the best article of food (*Counsels on Diet and Foods*, p. 333). On the same page she suggests the use of fruit in place of rich pastries, cakes and desserts, etc."

He goes on to point out that in Ellen White's diary of 1872 "she writes of their being in Colorado, and she stated that for breakfast they had green peas, green corn, gems and pears.

87

Apparently there was no problem to her in the combination of these foods, but there might be to some people. . . .

"In minute matters of diet," he concluded, the application of Ellen White's counsels "may differ in the experience of different individuals and this would be based somewhat on individual tolerance to certain foods or combination of foods. What might be unwise for one might not be a serious matter for another" (A. L. White to O. Willhelm, May 13, 1966).

The literary context makes a difference. That is true on the issue of eating fruits and vegetables at the same meal, which she ties to the qualifier of feeble digestion in her most basic statements on the topic.

Another illustration where literary context makes a difference is in relation to Ellen White's often-quoted statement that "Christ is waiting with longing desire for the manifestation of Himself in His church. When the character of Christ shall be perfectly reproduced in His people, then He will come to claim them as His own" (COL 69).

Too many people have read that statement without carefully examining its literary context. As a result, they have imputed meanings to it about perfection not found in its literary framework. They not only "rip" the *Christ's Object Lessons* statement from its context, but they isolate other statements from such books as *Counsels on Diet and Foods* and the *Testimonies* from their backgrounds and create a distorted and even dangerous theology. That method has led many readers (including me) off on a self-destructive tangent in their Christian experience.

Such readers could have avoided a lot of problems if they would have more carefully read the preceding two pages of the *Christ's Object Lessons* statement. Ellen White plainly states that Christ seeks to reproduce Himself in the hearts of others, and that those who have accepted Him will put away the self-centered living of Satan's kingdom. They will be becoming more like Christ because they have received "the Spirit of Christ—the Spirit of unselfish love and labor for others." As a result, she says, "your love [will] be made perfect. More and more you will reflect the likeness of Christ in all that is pure, noble, and lovely" (COL 67, 68). Thus perfectly reproducing the character of Christ in its literary context is not a call to monastic withdrawal, but a call for us to let Jesus live out His love in our daily lives.

The literary context makes all the difference in the world in understanding such statements. Unfortunately, even the "official" compilations at times print such statements without their all-important literary framework (see, for example, LDE 39). And while that is understandable, given the purpose and spatial limitations of all compilations, the existence of such instances highlights the need to go back to the original source wherever available so as to come as close to Ellen White's true meaning as possible. The fact that official compilations give the reference to the original source makes this easier. The study of literary contexts is not an optional luxury on important statements—it is a crucial part of faithfully reading Ellen White's writings.

It is impossible to overestimate the importance of studying Ellen White's articles and books in their contexts rather than merely reading topical compilations or selecting out quotations on this or that topic through the use of the *Comprehensive Index* to her writings or the White Estate's CD-ROM, *The Published Ellen G. White Writings.* Such approaches, if used exclusively, would make the *Index* and the CD-ROM disk the worst thing that ever happened to Ellen White studies. Such tools have their places, but we should use them in connection with broad reading that helps us to be more aware not only of the literary context of Ellen White's statements but also of the overall balance in her writings.

Chapter Fourteen

Recognize Ellen White's Understanding of the Ideal and the Real

Ellen White often found herself plagued by "those who," she claimed, "select from the testimonies the strongest expressions and, without bringing in or making any account of the circumstances under which the cautions and warnings are given, make them of force in every case. . . . Picking out some things in the testimonies they drive them upon every one, and disgust rather than win souls" (3SM 285, 286).

Her observation not only highlights the fact that we need to take the historical context of Ellen White's statements into consideration when reading her counsel, but also indicates that she put some statements in stronger or more forceful language than others. That idea leads us to the concept of the ideal and the real in Mrs. White's writings.

When Ellen White is stating the ideal, she often uses her strongest language. It is as if she needs to speak loudly in order to be heard. One such statement appears in *Fundamentals of Christian Education*. "*Never,*" she exhorted, "can the proper education be given to the youth in this country, *or any other country,* unless they are separated a *wide distance from the cities*" (p. 312; italics supplied).

Now, that is about as forceful a statement as she could have made. Not only is it adamant, but it appears to imply universality in terms of time and space. There is no stronger word than "never." In its strictest meaning it allows no exceptions. She uses the same sort of powerful, unbending language in terms of location—"in this country, or any other country." Once again a plain reading of the words permits no exceptions. We are dealing with what appears to be a universal prohibition regarding the building of schools in cities. But the statement is stronger than that. Such schools are not merely to be out of the cities, but "separated a wide distance" from them.

Here is inflexible language that does not suggest any exceptions.

At this point it is important to examine the historical context in which she made the statement. According to the reference supplied in the book, this counsel was first published in 1894 (see FE 327). The introductory statement to the article on page 310 indicates that she was speaking about the choice of where to locate "the Australian Bible School" (later known as the Avondale School or Avondale College).

Prior to the development of the Avondale School, Adventist colleges had left much to be desired. The first official Adventist school had been established in Battle Creek, Michigan, during the early 1870s. Battle Creek College featured a classical curriculum that had little room for the study of the Bible and even less space for practical training for the world of work. Beyond that, it huddled in the city of Battle Creek on less than 10 acres. Other major Adventist schools in North America begun during the 1880s largely followed the Battle Creek pattern.

In the development of the Avondale School, Ellen White hoped to start a new approach to Adventist education. As a result, she urged the opening of a school that would emphasize Bible study, missionary outreach, and practical training, while at the same time removing the dominance of the "pagan" classics with their focus on the ancient Greek and Latin authors. She also urged, as we read above, that the school be rural. The result was a school founded near the little village of Cooranbong on 1,450 acres of farmland. As counseled by Ellen White, the founders of the school had established it a "wide distance" from the cities.

Ellen White was overjoyed with the new institution. In varying contexts she later referred to Avondale as an "object lesson," a "sample school," a "model school," and a "pattern" (LS 374; letter 88, 1900; MS 186, 1898; CT 349). In 1900 she categorically stated that "the school in Avondale is to be a pattern for other schools which shall be established among our people" (MS 92, 1900).

And Avondale did become a model for Adventist schools around the world. Battle Creek College sold its few acres and began again as Emmanuel Missionary College (now Andrews University) in Berrien Springs, Michigan, while Healdsburg College in California left its town location to move to the top of Howell Mountain, where it became Pacific Union College. Both were separated a "wide distance" from any cities. Beyond those schools, new educational institutions also generally followed the Avondale pattern of large acreages in rural sites.

But there were exceptions. For example, by 1909 the Adventist work in large cities was increasing. And those cities had families who could not afford to send their children to rural institutions. As a result, Ellen White counseled the building of schools in the cities. *"So far as possible,"* we read, ". . . schools should be established outside the cities. *But* in the cities there are many children who could not attend schools away from the cities; and for the benefit of these, schools should be opened in the cities as well as in the country" (9T 201; italics supplied).

By this time you may be asking yourself how the same woman could claim that proper education could "never" be given in Australia "or any other country, unless they [schools] are separated a wide distance from the cities" (FE 312) and yet still advocate the establishment of schools in the cities.

The answer is that rural education for all children was the *ideal* that the church should aim at "so far as possible." But the truth is that the hard facts of life make such education impossible for some. Thus *reality* dictated a compromise if Christian education were to reach children from poorer families. Ellen White understood and accepted the tension between the ideal and the real.

Unfortunately, many of her readers fail to take that fact into consideration. They focus merely on Mrs. White's "strongest" statements, those that express the ideal, and ignore the moderating passages. As a result, as we noted above, "picking out some things in the testimonies they drive them upon every one, and disgust rather than win souls" (3SM 286).

Ellen White has more balance than many of her so-called followers. Genuine followers must take into account her understanding of the tension between the ideal and the real in applying her counsel.

Another illustration of the flexibility in Ellen White's writings has to do with the founding of the new Washington Training College (now Columbia Union College) early in the twentieth century. The school and the adjoining Washington Sanitarium shared 50 acres at the outskirts of the nation's capital. Each institution had about 25 acres. Not only was the school built on a small acreage, but it was not separated a "wide distance" from the city. Thus the school hardly followed the Avondale pattern.

Yet Ellen White could tell the Adventist people that "the securing of this land was in the Lord's providence." A few days later she wrote, "The location that has been secured for our school and sanitarium is all that could be desired. The land resembles representations that have been shown me by the Lord. . . . There is on it ample room for a school and a sanitarium, without crowding either institution" (LS 397).

We might ask, "How can this be?" It seems almost like a contradiction of principle. Before we become too hasty, however, we should point out that she claimed that "it is well adapted for the *purpose* for which it is to be used" (*ibid.;* italics supplied).

The word "purpose" is the key word to note. The Washington school at that early date had a different goal than that of Avondale and several other Adventist educational institutions. Thus it also had a different set of conditions for its location.

Ellen White utilized a great deal of flexibility in applying her counsels. In another connection she penned that "it would be a sad mistake for us to fail to consider thoroughly the purpose for which each of our schools is established" (CT 203, 204). She was far from being rigid. Thus, in spite of her high regard for the Avondale pattern, she could state in 1901 that "the Lord has not designed any one, special, exact plan in education" (3SM 227). Again, in 1907 she wrote regarding the Madison School, which was doing its best to follow the Avondale "pattern" under Adventism's most zealous educational reformers, that "no exact pattern can be given for the establishment of schools in new fields. The climate, the surroundings, the condition of the country, and the means at hand with which to work must all bear a part in shaping the work" (CT 531).

In conclusion, it should be reiterated that Ellen White had more flexibility in interpreting her writings than many have realized. She was not only concerned with contextual factors in applying counsel to different situations, but also had a distinct understanding of the difference between God's ideal plan and the reality of the human situation that at times necessitated modification of the ideal. For that reason it is important that we don't just operate on the "strongest expressions" in her writings and seek to "drive them upon every one" (3SM 285, 286).

*

Chapter Fifteen

Use
Common Sense

Seventh-day Adventists have been known to differ and even argue over some of Ellen White's counsel. That situation is especially true of those statements that seem so straightforward and clear. One such statement appears in volume 3 of the *Testimonies:* "Parents should be the *only* teachers of their children until they have reached eight or ten years of age" (p. 137; italics supplied).

That passage is an excellent candidate for inflexible interpretation. After all, it is quite categorical. It offers no conditions and hints at no exceptions. Containing no "ifs," "ands," "ors," or "buts" to modify its impact, it just plainly states as fact that "parents should be the *only* teachers of their children until they have reached eight or ten years of age." Mrs. White first published the statement in 1872. The fact that it reappeared in her writings in 1882 and 1913 undoubtedly had the effect of strengthening what appears to be its unconditional nature.

Interestingly enough, however, a struggle over that statement has provided us with perhaps the very best record we possess of how Mrs. White interpreted her own writings.

The Adventists living near the St. Helena Sanitarium in northern California had built a church school in 1902. The older children attended it, while some careless Adventist parents let their younger children run freely in the neighborhood without proper training and discipline. Some of the school board members believed that they should build a classroom for the younger children, but others held that it would be wrong to do so, because Ellen White had plainly stated that "parents should be the *only* teachers of their children until they have reached eight or ten years of age."

One faction on the board apparently felt that it was more important to give some help to the neglected children than to hold to the letter of the law. The other faction believed that it had an inflexible command, some "straight testimony" that it must obey.

To put it mildly, the issue split the school board. Now the most interesting fact in this case is that the school was situated on Ellen White's property. Thus the board was able to request an interview with her to discuss the question of school-age attendance and the responsibility of the church for the education of its young children. Fortunately, the entire interview was transcribed, typed out, and preserved in Ellen White's manuscript file (see MS 7, 1904—much of it has been reproduced in 3SM 214-226).

The interview itself is one of the most remarkable documents in the Ellen White corpus of writings. It clearly demonstrates some of the principles Ellen White used in interpreting her own counsels in a real-life situation. *It is a document that every student of her writings should read.*

Early in the interview Mrs. White reaffirmed her position that the family should ideally be the school for young children. "The home," she said, "is both a family church and a family school" (3SM 214). That is the ideal that one finds throughout her writings. The institutional church and school are there to supplement the work of a healthy family. That is the ideal.

But, as we discovered in the previous chapter, the ideal is not always the real. Or, to say it in other words, reality is often less than ideal. Thus Ellen White continued in the interview: "Mothers *should* be able to instruct their little ones wisely during the earlier years of childhood. *If* every mother were capable of doing this, *and would* take time to teach her children the lessons they should learn in early life, *then* all children could be kept in the home school until they are eight, or nine, or ten years old" *(ibid.* 214, 215; italics supplied).

Here we begin to find Mrs. White dealing with a reality that modifies the categorical and unconditional nature of her statement on parents being the only teachers of their children until 8 or 10 years of age. The ideal is that mothers "should" be able to function as the best teachers. But realism intrudes when Ellen White uses such words as "if" and "then." She definitely implies that not all mothers are capable and that not all are willing. But "if" they are both capable and willing, "then all children could be kept in the home school."

Her realism continues as the interview progresses. Unfortunately, she noted, many did not take their responsibilities seriously. It would have been best if they had not become parents. But since they had unwisely brought children into the world, the church should not stand by idly without giving any guidance to the children's characters. She held that the Christian community had a responsibility to train such neglected ones, and she even went so far as to claim that the church needed to reform its ideas in regard to establishing kindergartens.

During the interview she remarked that "God desires us to deal with these problems sensibly" *(ibid.* 215). Ellen White became quite stirred up with those readers who took an inflexible attitude toward her writings and sought to follow the letter of her message while missing the underlying principles. She evidenced disapproval of both the words and attitudes of her rigid interpreters when she declared: *"My mind has been greatly stirred in regard to the idea, 'Why, Sister White has said so and so, and Sister White has said so and so; and therefore we are going right up to it.'"* She then added that *"God wants us all to have common sense, and He wants us to reason from common sense. Circumstances alter conditions. Circumstances change the relation of things"* *(ibid.* 217; italics supplied). Ellen White was anything but inflexible in interpreting her own writings, and it is a point of the first magnitude that we realize that fact.

Part of the problem is that we "grab" an Ellen White quote merely because it is clear and forceful and push it into situations in which it does not apply. In the process we not only at times contradict Christian principles, but we make nonsense out of the counsel itself and offend people. Thus her impassioned utterance about those who have taken one of her statements and "are going right up to it." She had no doubt that the mindless use of her ideas could be harmful. Thus it is little wonder that she said that "God wants us all to have common sense" in using extracts from her writings, even when she phrased those extracts in the strongest and most unconditional language.

Perhaps one of the most deadly breaches of the commonsense rule in applying Ellen White's counsel took place at the Solusi school in what is now Zimbabwe. The first missionaries arrived on the Solusi campus in 1894. Taking Ellen White's counsel on avoiding harmful drugs seriously and inflexibly, they, as faithful health reformers, refused to take quinine during a major outbreak of malaria in 1898. The result: of the original seven who had arrived in 1894, only three were still alive, and two of those were at the Cape recovering from malaria. The remaining missionary had been the "unfaithful" one. He had used quinine on the basis that using some of a harmful drug was better than remaining vulnerable to the full force of the disease. In short, he employed common sense in the face of a serious reality that negated the absolute ideal. As a result, he continued to serve and witness at Solusi.

I still remember visiting the graves of those "faithful" health reformers at Solusi. As I stood with my head bowed, I realized as never before the serious consequences of not following Ellen White's counsel to use common sense in the application of inspired counsel.

It is of interest that Ellen White was at one time approached by a South Pacific missionary who had lost his oldest son to malaria because he had refused to give him quinine based on her counsel on quinine and other drugs.

" 'Would I have sinned,' " he asked her, " 'to give the boy quinine when I knew of no other way to check malaria and when the prospect was that he would die without it?' In reply she said, 'No, we are expected to do the best we can'" (2SM 282n).

While the deadly results of not applying common sense in the physical realm are immediately evident to all, only eternity will hold the record of the damage done by those who have inflexibly and nonsensically pushed Ellen White (and biblical) quotations to their logical extremes in the realm of the spirit and who eventually "disgusted" people and drove them away from the God they had projected by their extremism (see 3SM 285-287). We will return to that topic in our final chapter.

Chapter Sixteen

Discover the
Underlying Principles

In July 1894 Ellen White sent a letter to the denomination's headquarters church in Battle Creek, Michigan, in which she condemned the purchase and riding of bicycles (8T 50-53). At first glance it appears strange that such an issue should be considered important enough for a prophet to deal with. It seems especially odd when we note that the bicycle issue had been specifically revealed in vision.

How should we apply such counsel today? Does it mean that Seventh-day Adventists should not own bicycles?

In answering that question we first need to examine the historical context, as recommended in chapter 12. In 1894 the modern bicycle was just beginning to be manufactured, and a fad quickly developed to acquire bicycles, not for the purpose of economical transportation, but simply to be in style, to enter bicycle races, and to parade around town on them. In the evening such parading included the hanging of Japanese lanterns on the bicycles. Bicycling was the in thing—the thing to do if you were anything or anybody on the social scale.

Extracts from an article entitled "When All the World Went Wheeling" will help us get into the historical context of the bicycle counsel. "Toward the end of the last century," we read, "the

American people were swept with a consuming passion which left them with little time or money for anything else. . . . What was this big new distraction? For an answer the merchants had only to look out the window and watch their erstwhile customers go whizzing by. America had discovered the bicycle, and everybody was making the most of the new freedom it brought. . . . The bicycle began as a rich man's toy. Society and celebrity went awheel. . . .

"The best early bicycle cost $150, an investment comparable to the cost of an automobile today. . . . Every member of the family wanted a 'wheel,' and entire family savings often were used up in supplying the demand" *(Reader's Digest,* December 1951).

In a similar vein social historian J. C. Furnas notes that "one of the sights of Garden City, Long Island, in the early 1890s was the elegant Mrs. Burke-Roche in her gray-and-white cycling costume on her silver-plated bicycle. The flashier one that Lillian Russell rode in Central Park had gold trim" *(The Americans,* p. 810).

In the light of the historical context, Ellen White's statement in 1894 regarding bicycles takes on a new significance. "There seemed to be," she wrote, "a bicycle craze. Money was spent to gratify an enthusiasm in this direction that might better, far better, have been invested in building houses of worship where they are greatly needed. . . . A bewitching influence seemed to be passing as a wave over our people. . . . Satan works with intensity of purpose to induce our people to invest their time and money in gratifying supposed wants. This is a species of idolatry. . . . While hundreds are starving for bread, while famine and pestilence are seen and felt, . . . shall those who profess to love and serve God act as did the people in the days of Noah, following the imagination of their hearts? . . .

"There were some who were striving for the mastery, each trying to excel the other in the swift running of their bicycles. There was a spirit of strife and contention among them as to which should be the greatest. . . . Said my Guide: 'These things are an offense to God. Both near and afar off souls are perishing for the bread of life and the water of salvation.' When Satan is defeated in one line, he will be all ready with other schemes and plans which will appear attractive and needful, and which will absorb money and thought, and encourage selfishness, so that he can overcome those who are so easily led into a false and selfish indulgence."

"What burden," she asks, "do these persons carry for the advancement of the work of God? . . . Is this investment of means and this spinning of bicycles through the streets of Battle Creek giving evidence of the genuineness of your faith in the last solemn warning to be given to human beings standing on the very verge of the eternal world?" (8T 51, 52).

Her counsel on bicycles is obviously dated. Within a few years bicycles became quite inexpensive and were relegated to the realm of practical transportation for young people and those without means, even as the larger culture switched its focus and desires to the four-wheeled successor of the humble bicycle.

That social transformation left the counsel on bicycles without practical application. Or did it? While it is true that some of the specifics of the counsel no longer apply, the principles on which the specific counsel rests remain quite applicable across time and space.

And what are some of those principles? First, that Christians are not to spend money on selfish gratification. Second, that Christians are not to strive for mastery over one another by doing things that generate a spirit of strife and contention. Third, that Christians should focus their primary values on the kingdom to come and on helping others during the present period of history. And fourth, that Satan will always have a scheme to derail Christians into the realm of selfish indulgence.

Those principles are unchangeable. They apply to every place and to every age of earthly history. Bicycles were merely the point of contact between the principles and the human situation in Battle Creek during 1894. The particulars of time and place change, but the universal principles remain constant.

Our responsibility as Christians is not only to read God's counsel to us, but to apply it faithfully to our personal lives. Our first task, therefore, is to seek out the principles of Christian living through a Spirit-guided study of the Bible and the writings of Ellen White.

Our second task is to relate the principles we have found to our personal lives and social context. To do so, we must have some understanding of the historic situation that originally called forth the counsel. That information will enable us to differentiate between the universal principles underlying the inspired statement and the particulars that it suggested to deal with a problem in a historic time and place.

Third, we must have a good grasp of the current situation to which we are going to apply the universal principles. Only with such understanding can we intelligently put into practice the prophetic principles in our daily lives, our schools and churches, and in the larger culture.

Application must not take place without understanding. But understanding implies the use of reason and common sense, as we saw in chapter 15. A central problem that all of us face is that of balance between faith in inspired documents and our God-given reason. One polar extreme is to rely unthinkingly on prophetic authority (the "I have a quote" approach to solving every issue), while the other is to lean on rationality in an unhealthy manner that allows it to become a rationalization or excuse for what we really wanted to do anyway. Inspired counsel must always guide our rational understanding. On the other hand, we must always comprehend and apply the truth of that counsel through the aid of our rationality.

To rely on either inspired writings or rational understanding without the other is a fatal misconception. Authoritative revelation and sanctified reason go hand in hand as we seek to understand God and put His wisdom into practice in our daily lives. God gave us the power of rational thought, and He expects us to use it for His glory (Isa. 1:18; Ed 17). Inspired counsel supplies the basic principles that set the bounds and direction for our rational thinking, while the thinking itself enables us to apply that counsel to our unique and ever-changing situations.

Christian living is a dynamic experience inseparably linked to common sense and thinking and acting upon one's thoughts. Christianity is therefore a moral enterprise in which individuals have responsibility in the eyes of God. Rigidity and inflexibility of thought and action are the antithesis of living Christianity. The Christian's task is to search out God's revelations and then to seek to put them into practice in daily living without doing violence to the intent of their underlying principles. That takes personal dedication as well as sensitivity to the guidance of the Holy Spirit.

It was in connection with the living Spirit that Ellen White lived and sought to guide the Adventist Church. Jesus, who in His flexible manner was able to meet all classes of people, exemplified that same stance. His adaptable-yet-principle-based life and teachings burst the old wineskins of pharisaism.

It might be added that the Sermon on the Mount is an excellent example of some of the ideas set forth in this chapter. Jesus in each of the six illustrations at the end of Matthew 5 sought to lead His hearers to the heart of the principle of the law and to applying it to their own lives.

Chapter Seventeen

Realize That Inspiration Is Not Infallible, Inerrant, or Verbal

I was led to conclude and most firmly believe that *every* word that you ever spoke in public or private, that *every* letter you wrote under *any* and *all* circumstances, was as inspired as the ten commandments. I held that view with *absolute* tenacity against innumerable objections raised to it by many who were occupying prominent positions in the [Adventist] cause," wrote Dr. David Paulson to Ellen White on April 19, 1906. Deeply concerned over the nature of Ellen White's inspiration, Paulson wondered whether he should continue to hold such a rigid view. In the process he raised the question of verbal inspiration and the related issues of infallibility and inerrancy. Since a correct understanding of such issues is of crucial importance in reading Ellen White and/or the Bible, we will examine each of them in this chapter.

Mrs. White replied to Paulson on June 14, 1906. "My brother," she penned, "you have studied my writings diligently, and you have never found that I have made any such claims [to verbal inspiration], neither will you find that the pioneers in our cause ever made such claims" for her writings. She went on to illustrate inspiration in her writings by referring to the inspiration of the Bible writers. Even though God had inspired the biblical truths, they were "expressed in the words of men." She saw the

Bible as representing "a union of the divine and the human." Thus "the testimony is conveyed through the imperfect expression of human language, yet it is the testimony of God" (1SM 24-26).

Such sentiments represent Ellen White's consistent witness across time. "The Bible," she wrote in 1886, "is written by inspired men, but it is not God's mode of thought and expression. It is that of humanity. God, as a writer, is not represented. . . . The writers of the Bible were God's penmen, not His pen. . . .

"It is not the words of the Bible that are inspired, but the men that were inspired. Inspiration acts not on the man's words or his expressions but on the man himself, who, under the influence of the Holy Ghost, is imbued with thoughts. But the words receive the impress of the individual mind. The divine mind is diffused. The divine mind and will is combined with the human mind and will; thus the utterances of the man are the word of God" *(ibid.* 21).

That statement is about as clear and insightful as can be found anywhere on the subject of verbal versus thought inspiration. Of her own experience she wrote, "Although I am as dependent upon the Spirit of the Lord in writing my views as I am in receiving them, yet the words I employ in describing what I have seen are my own, unless they be those spoken to me by an angel, which I always enclose in marks of quotation" *(ibid.* 37).

The position she espoused on thought versus verbal inspiration was the one officially accepted by the denomination at its 1883 General Conference session. "We believe," reads part of the resolution, "the light given by God to his servants is by the enlightenment of the mind, thus imparting the thoughts, and not (except in rare cases) the very words in which the ideas should be expressed" (RH, Nov. 27, 1883).

Yet that position was more easily voted upon than fully accepted. Thus W. C. White would later write that the theory of verbal inspiration infiltrated Adventism during the latter part of the nineteenth century. Its acceptance, he added, "has resulted in bringing into our work questions and perplexities without end, and always increasing" (3SM 454).

We see the problematic nature of the issue illustrated in the life of D. M. Canright, at one time a leading minister in the denomination, but its foremost critic between 1887 and 1919. Canright bitterly opposed Ellen White. His 1919 book against her asserted that "every line she wrote, whether in articles, letters, testimonies or books, she claimed was dictated to her by the Holy Ghost, and hence must be infallible" (*Life of Mrs. E. G. White,* p. 9).

We have seen above that Ellen White herself took just the opposite position, but that didn't stop the damage being done by those with a false theory of inspiration.

Not only did it affect those who rejected Adventism and Ellen White's gift partly because of their rigid views of inspiration (such as Canright and A. T. Jones), but a mistaken belief in verbalism also distorted the views of many who remained at the heart of the church. Thus W. C. White wrote to S. N. Haskell in 1911 that *"there is danger of our injuring Mother's work by claiming for it more than she claims for it,* more than Father ever claimed for it, more than Elders Andrews, [J. H.] Waggoner, or Smith ever claimed for it. I cannot see consistency in our putting forth a claim of verbal inspiration when Mother does not make any such claim" (W. C. White to S. N. Haskell, Oct. 31, 1912; italics supplied).

Haskell replied to White two months later, claiming that W. C. White's view of inspiration was "laying a foundation for a tremendous shaking on the Testimonies." Haskell went on to argue that "those men who are the strongest [in the faith] are those who have had the most unlimited confidence in your mother's writings, and those who ride in a shifting seat are the ones who sooner or later take the front seat, and believe the Testimonies, or a back seat, and give them up and apostatize" (S. N. Haskell to W. C. White, Jan. 8, 1913).

White pushed his point again a week after Haskell penned his letter. Mrs. White's son noted that he was "aware that there are a large number of leading men who are determined to stand loyally to the Testimonies, and that some of these feel that one of the most serious difficulties in holding their brethren loyal to the Testimonies is the fact that a few men of age and experience [such as Haskell] insist upon pressing on them the theory of verbal inspiration which Mother does not stand for, which the General Conference does not stand for, which my father never stood for. Some have expressed the opinion to me that the extreme and extravagant positions taken by a few men, including yourself, are doing more to bring the shaking over the Testimonies than any other one element in the work" (W. C. White to S. N. Haskell, Jan. 15, 1913).

The tragedy of the interchange between W. C. White and Haskell is that Haskell advocated a position that Ellen White explicitly rejected in her postscript to one of her son's letters to Haskell. On a carbon copy of the October 31 letter to Haskell quoted above, the letter in which Willie stated in no uncertain terms that Haskell and others were injuring her work by claiming too much for her writings, she wrote, "I approve of the remarks made in this letter." She then signed her name. It was unfortunate that Haskell never saw that note. Quite probably W. C. White never saw it himself, since several carbon copies of that letter existed. If he had seen the copy with her postscript it would have been natural to send it to Haskell as a clincher to the argument. But he didn't.

Unfortunately, the argument for verbal inspiration continued on into the 1920s. Thus B. L. House could argue in his denominationally sponsored *Analytical Studies in Bible Doctrines for Seventh-day Adventist Colleges* (1926) that the selection of "the very words of Scripture in the original languages was overruled by the Holy Spirit" (p. 66).

That position, of course, is the very one Ellen White had rejected in theory and practice throughout her ministry. W. C. White spoke to the issue of verbal inspiration when some questioned the revising of *The Great Controversy* in 1911. "Mother," he told the General Conference delegates, "has never laid claim to verbal inspiration" and neither did the other founders of Adventism. White set forth an unanswerable challenge when he asked, "If there were verbal inspiration in writing her manuscripts, why should there be on her part the work of addition or adaptation? It is a fact that Mother often takes one of her manuscripts, and goes over it thoughtfully, making additions that develop the thought still further" (3SM 437).

It is unfortunate that the struggle did not end with the attempts of W. C. White and his mother to set the issue straight. In spite of the clear statements of both, many today still hold to the verbalist position and its close relatives—inerrancy and false theories of infallibility. It is to those topics that we now turn.

In the realm of infallibility we again find some Adventists making much broader claims than those set forth by Ellen White. For example, a leading evangelist asserted in 1970 that "the very nature of our God demands an infallible Bible," that the Bible claims infallibility, and that "Jesus, heaven's glorious commander, accepted the Scriptures as unerring." He argued for a Bible that was perfectly free from any type of error. After all, he proposed, if the Bible was to err in any particular fact, "why should there not be errors of theology and of salvation as well?" *(Ministry,* January 1970, p. 6).

Before we go any further, perhaps we should define our terms. *Webster's New World Dictionary* describes "infallible" as "1. incapable of error; never wrong. 2. not liable to fail, go wrong, make a mistake, etc." It renders "inerrant" as "not erring, making no mistakes." It is essentially those definitions that many people *import* into the realm of the Bible and Ellen White's writings.

As to infallibility, Mrs. White plainly writes, "I never claimed it; God alone is infallible." Again she stated that "God and heaven alone are infallible" (1SM 37). While she claimed that "God's Word is infallible" *(ibid.* 416), we will see below that she did not mean that the Bible (or her writings) were free from error at all points.

To the contrary, in the introduction to *The Great Controversy* she sets forth her position quite concisely: "The Holy Scriptures are to be accepted as an authoritative, infallible revelation of His will" (p. vii). That is, the work of God's prophets is not infallible in all its details, but it is infallible in terms of revealing God's will to men and women. In a similar statement Ellen White commented that "His Word . . . is plain on every point essential to the salvation of the soul" (5T 706).

W. C. White treats the same issue when he observes: "Where she has followed the description of historians or the exposition of Adventist writers, *I believe that God has given her discernment to use that which is correct and in harmony with truth regarding all matters essential to salvation*. If it should be found by faithful study that she has followed some expositions of prophecy which in some detail regarding dates we cannot harmonize with our understanding of secular history, it does not influence my confidence in her writings as a whole any more than my confidence in the Bible is influenced by the fact that I cannot harmonize many of the statements regarding chronology" (3SM 449, 450; italics supplied).

I. Howard Marshall expands upon this insight when he writes that "the purpose of God in the composition of the Scriptures was to guide people to salvation and the associated way of life. From this statement we may surely conclude that God made the Bible all that it needs to be in order to achieve this purpose. It is in this sense that the word 'infallible' is properly applied to the Bible; it means that it is 'in itself a true and sufficient guide, which may be trusted implicitly.' . . . We may therefore suggest that 'infallible' means that the Bible is entirely trustworthy for the purposes for which God inspired it" (*Biblical Inspiration,* p. 53).

In summary, it appears that Mrs. White's use of the term *infallibility* has to do with the Bible being completely trustworthy as a guide to salvation. She doesn't mix that idea with the concept that the Bible or her writings are free from all possible errors of a factual nature.

Ellen White didn't beat around the bush on this topic. She openly acknowledged the possibility of errors in factual details in the Bible. "Some," she noted, "look to us gravely and say, 'Don't you think there might have been some mistake in the copyist or in the translators?' This is all probable, and the mind that is so narrow that it will hesitate and stumble over this possibility or probability would be just as ready to stumble over the mysteries of the Inspired Word, because their feeble minds cannot see through the purposes of God. . . . All the mistakes will not cause trouble to one soul, or cause any feet to stumble, that would not manufacture difficulties from the plainest revealed truth" (1SM 16).

Thus the faithful reader's belief is not shaken if he or she discovers that Matthew made a mistake in attributing a Messianic prophecy, written centuries before Christ's birth, to Jeremiah when it was actually Zechariah who inferred that Christ would be betrayed for 30 pieces of silver (see Matt. 27:9, 10; Zech. 11:12, 13). Nor will one be dismayed over the fact that 1 Samuel 16:10, 11 lists David as the eighth son of Jesse, but 1 Chronicles 2:15 refers to him as the seventh. Neither will faith be affected because the prophet Nathan wholeheartedly approved of King David's building of the Temple but the next day had to backtrack and tell David that God didn't want him to build it (see 2 Sam. 7; 1 Chron. 17). Prophets make mistakes.

The same kind of factual errors can be discovered in Ellen White's writings as are found in the Bible. The writings of God's prophets are infallible as a guide to salvation, but they are not inerrant or without error. Part of the lesson is that we need to read for the central lessons of Scripture and Ellen White rather than the details. We had something to say about that in chapter 7 and will have more on the topic of factual inerrancy in chapter 18.

What is important to remember at this point is that those who struggle over such problems as inerrancy and absolute infallibility are fighting a human-made problem. It is not anything that God ever claimed for the Bible or Ellen White ever claimed for the Bible or her writings. Inspiration for her had to do with the "practical purposes" (1SM 19) of human and divine relationships in the plan of salvation. We need to let God speak to us in His mode, rather than to superimpose our rules over God's prophets and then reject them if they don't live up to *our* expectations of what we think God should have done. Such an approach is a human invention that places our own authority over the Word of God. It makes us the judges of God and His Word. But such a position is not biblical; nor is it according to the way Ellen White has counseled the church. We need to read God's Word and Mrs. White's writings for the purpose for which He gave them and not let our modern concerns and definitions of purpose and accuracy come between us and His prophets.

C. S. Longacre, longtime religious liberty leader in the Seventh-day Adventist Church, has a lesson for us on this point. "You and some others who have made shipwreck of your faith in Mrs. White's testimonies," he wrote, "set up your standards of infallibility for her writings and what she said from time to time, which she never set up for herself or her writings, and because she did not measure up to those standards which you set up for her, you naturally throw her overboard and try to make her out as a false prophet. The trouble with A. T. Jones, the Ballengers," and others "who lost faith in Mrs. White's testimonies was that they took very extreme positions, and made a veritable deity and superwoman out of Mrs. White and all she ever said and wrote in any form and shape, and when she did not measure up to the 'straw man' or false standards they had set up for her in her private and personal correspondence and in offhand counsel she gave, then they lost faith and branded her as a false prophet. That is where most of the extremists on the Testimonies do end" (C. S. Longacre to W. A. Colcord, Dec. 10, 1929).

Chapter Eighteen

Avoid Making the Counsels "Prove" Things They Were Never Intended to Prove

In the previous chapter we noted that Ellen White did not claim verbal inspiration for her writings or the Bible, nor did she classify them as either inerrant or infallible in the sense of being free from factual mistakes. In spite of the efforts of Mrs. White and her son to move people away from too rigid a view of inspiration, many have continued on in that line.

The present chapter is an extension of the previous one. Down through the history of the denomination some have sought to use Ellen White's writings and the Bible for purposes for which God never intended them. Likewise, claims have been made for prophetic writings that transcend their purpose. Thus B. L. House approvingly cited another author to the effect that "'infallible guidance was given to those who wrote it [the Bible], so as to preserve them from error in the statement of facts'" in history and other areas (*Analytical Studies in Bible Doctrine,* p. 66). More recently an acquaintance of mine wrote that "all the claims that the Bible makes on any subject—theology, history, science, chronology, numbers, etc.—are absolutely trustworthy and dependable" (*Issues in Revelation and Inspiration,* p. 63).

Many would argue the same for Ellen White's writings. As a result, we find individuals who go to her writings to substantiate such things as historical facts and dates. Thus S. N. Haskell could write to Ellen White that he and his friends would "give more for one expression in your testimony than for all the histories you could stack between here and Calcutta" (S. N. Haskell to E. G. White, May 30, 1910).

Yet Ellen White never claimed that the Lord provided every historical detail in her works. To the contrary, she tells us that she generally went to the same sources available to us to get the historical facts that she used to fill out the outlines of the struggle between good and evil across the ages that she portrays so nicely in *The Great Controversy*. In regard to the writing of that volume, she wrote in its preface that "where a historian has so grouped together events as to afford, in brief, a comprehensive view of the subject, or has summarized details in a convenient manner, his words have been quoted; but in some instances no specific credit has been given, since the quotations are not given for the purpose of citing that writer as authority, but because his statement affords a ready and forcible presentation of the subject." Her purpose in such books as *The Great Controversy* was "not so much . . . to present new truths concerning the struggles of former times, as to bring out facts and principles which have a bearing on coming events" (GC xii).

That statement of purpose is crucial in understanding her use of history. Her intention was to trace the dynamics of the conflict between good and evil across time. That was her message. The historical facts merely enriched its tapestry. She was not seeking to provide incontrovertible historical data. In actuality, as she put it, the "facts" she used were "well known and universally acknowledged by the Protestant world" (*ibid.* xi).

When anyone challenged the accuracy of the facts she employed, she had no hesitancy in changing them in new editions of her books. An example is the case of the bell that signaled the beginning of the destruction of tens of thousands of Protestants on the Day of Saint Bartholomew in 1572. In the 1888 edition of *The Great Controversy* (p. 272) she mentioned in passing that it was the palace bell of King Charles IX that began the massacre. But subsequent historians suggested that it was really the church bell of St. Germain, across the street from the palace, while still other historians claimed it was the bell of the Palace of Justice.

The revised 1911 edition of *Great Controversy* redrafted the statement to read simply, "A bell, tolling at dead of night, was a signal for the slaughter" (GC 272). The identity of the bell was not the issue—it was the events of that night that were important. The same can be said for other factual changes made in the 1911 revision.

What is true of Ellen White's use of facts in postbiblical church history is also true of her practice when writing of the biblical period. As a result, she could ask her sons that they request "Mary [Willie's wife] to find me some histories of the Bible that would give me the order of events. I have nothing and can find nothing in the library here" (E. G. White to W. C. White and J. E. White, Dec. 22, 1885).

"Regarding Mother's writings," W. C. White told Haskell, *"she has never wished our brethren to treat them as authority on history.* When 'Great Controversy' was first written, she often times gave a partial description of some scene presented to her, and when Sister Davis [her editorial assistant] made inquiry regarding time and place, Mother referred her to what was already written in the books of Elder Smith and in secular histories. *When 'Controversy' was written, Mother never thought that the readers would take it as an authority on historical dates and use it to settle controversies, and she does not now feel that it ought to be used in that way.* Mother regards with the greatest respect those faithful historians who have given their life to the study of the working out in this world's history of God's great plan, and who have found in this study a correspondence of . . . history with prophecy" (W. C. White to S. N. Haskell, Oct. 31, 1912; italics supplied; cf. 3SM 446, 447).

It was in that same letter that Willie warned Haskell "that there is danger of our injuring Mother's work by claiming for it more than she claims for it." And, as we saw in chapter 17, after Mrs. White read this letter she appended a note saying, *"I approve of the remarks made in this letter"* and signed her name (*ibid.;* italics supplied).

Twenty years later W. C. White wrote that "in our conversations with her [Ellen White] regarding the truthfulness and the accuracy of what she had quoted from historians, she expressed confidence in the historians from whom she had drawn, but never would consent to the course pursued by a few men who took her writings as a standard and endeavored by the use of them to prove the correctness of one historian as against the correctness of another. From this I gained the impression that the principal use of the passage quoted from historians was not to make a new history, not to correct errors in history, but to use valuable illustrations to make plain important spiritual truths.

"If our brethren will endeavor to get from the writings of Sister White that which she endeavored to put into them, if they will abandon the plan of trying to use them in argumentative contention, much blessing will come to us all" (W. C. White to L. E. Froom, Feb. 18, 1932).

Not only do we need to avoid using Ellen White to "prove" the details of history, but the same caution must be expressed in the realm of the details of science. In saying this I do not mean to imply that there is not a great deal of accuracy in the scientific inferences of Ellen White's writings—and the Bible's, for that matter—but that we must not seek to prove this and that scientific detail from them.

Let me illustrate. Some claim that John Calvin, the great sixteenth-century Reformer, resisted Copernicus's discovery that the earth rotated around the sun by quoting Psalm 93:1: "The world also is stablished; that it cannot be moved." In a similar vein, many have pointed out that the Bible talks about the four corners of the earth and the fact that the sun "comes up" and "goes down." In such cases, the Bible is merely making incidental remarks rather than setting forth scientific doctrine.

To take another illustration, one can only imagine the difficulties we could get into if we tried to use the Bible to "prove" in twentieth-century terms that rabbits or hares "chew the cud" (Deut. 14:7). It seems that Adventist leader W. A. Colcord was correct when he wrote that "natural history [science] gives us to understand that the hare does not chew the cud, but simply wobbles its jaws after the fashion of animals which do chew the cud" (W. A. Colcord to B. F. Purdham, July 6, 1892).

We find another illustration in Ellen White's *Education*, where she notes that not only the moon but the stars shine by the reflected light of the sun. Rather than seeing this as a new scientific discovery or, on the other hand, a serious scientific error, it seems to me that we should regard it as an offhand remark that she used in illustrating a very valid point. Remember, it is the point that counts, not the illustration.

Let's examine the quotation in its context: "We can trace the line of the world's teachers as far back as human records extend; but the Light was before them. As the moon and the stars of our solar system shine by the reflected light of the sun, so, as far as their teaching is true, do the world's great thinkers reflect the rays of the Sun of Righteousness. Every gleam of thought, every flash of the intellect, is from the Light of the world" (Ed 13, 14). Her point is not only clear, but it is valid. God is the ultimate source of all truth. We need to remember to focus on the center of what God's prophets are telling us rather than on the edges (see chapter 7).

One final illustration from Ellen White's experience should help us be duly cautious in seeking to prove scientific details from her writings. Joseph Bates, who cofounded the Seventh-day Adventist Church with James and Ellen White, early on doubted the genuineness of Ellen's prophetic ministry. The turning point for Bates came after a vision at Topsham, Maine, in November 1846 in which she provided astronomical information that she had no way of knowing. Bates, an ex-seaman who kept up on astronomy, afterward questioned her knowledge of the field. Finding her quite ill-informed, he came to the conclusion that God had indeed given her facts in vision regarding the most up-to-date astronomical knowledge. After that experience he was a firm believer in Ellen White's ministry.

My point here is that the information provided in vision was not the final word on the full number of moons for the planets that Bates believed were in question. Rather it provided information that related to the number of heavenly bodies that could be seen through telescopes in 1846. Stronger, more modern telescopes have brought into view additional moons circling the planets Bates assumed she was describing. Yet if Ellen White had been shown what our stronger telescopes now reveal, what she said would have confirmed rather than dispelled Bates's doubts. The vision paralleled the known data for that time rather than absolute scientific fact. It is evident that God's purpose in this experience was to establish confidence in the visions in the mind of Bates. It would be quite foolish to seek to prove the absolute number of moons circling certain planets from such data.

Remember that the Bible and Ellen White's writings are not intended to be divine encyclopedias for things scientific and historical. Rather they are to reveal our human hopelessness and then point us to the solution in salvation through Jesus. In the process, God's revelation provides a framework in which we can understand the bits and pieces of historical and scientific knowledge gained through other lines of study.

Make Sure
Ellen White Said It

What do you think," asked a man in the audience, "about Mrs. White's statement concerning the importance of giving special study to the 144,000 before the close of probation?"

Fortunately, I knew the answer to that one. She said just the opposite—that it wasn't necessary and that we ought to focus our energies on studying those things clearly taught in the Bible (see 1SM 174, 175). In short, she *never* said that it would be important to study the identity of the 144,000 before the close of probation.

That statement, along with many others, is a part of the Ellen G. White apocrypha. *What,* you may be thinking, *is the Ellen G. White apocrypha?* It is those statements or sentiments attributed to her authorship but for which no documentation is known to exist, and which it is believed she did not utter.

A fair number of such statements are in circulation that apparently have been falsely attributed to Ellen White. How can we identify such statements? The first clue that they are apocryphal for those who are familiar with Ellen White's writings is that such statements are often out of harmony with the general tenor of her thought. That is, they seem strange when compared to the bulk of her ideas, appear to be out of place in her mouth. Strangeness, of course, is not proof that we are dealing with an apocryphal statement. It is merely an indication.

The safest way to test the authenticity of an Ellen White statement is to ask for the reference to its source. Once we know where it is found, we can check to see if Ellen White said it and also examine the wording and context to determine if it has been interpreted correctly.

Often in weekend seminars I am asked questions about Ellen White statements that sound strange to me. The only thing I can tell the questioners is to supply me with the reference and I will examine it and write or phone them on the topic. Generally they have no reference, because one doesn't exist. But sometimes they have a source reference, such as the *Review and Herald,* July 24, 1895, p. 30. Such citations sound impressive because of their precision. But it is also true that they are often not genuine, or the statement has been read through biased eyes or quoted incorrectly so as to give it a different meaning than what Ellen White intended.

How do such apocryphal statements come into existence? Arthur White suggests at least five ways in the *Comprehensive Index to the Writings of Ellen G. White:* (1) faulty memory, (2) an incorrect association of ideas, (3) excerpts taken out of their setting, (4) writings falsely attributed, and (5) pure fiction (3:3189-3192).

Such mistakes may be sincere and accidental, or they may be, in a few cases, malicious and purposeful. But all of them are misleading.

Like most issues treated in this book, this one also came up in Mrs. White's lifetime. Her fullest treatment of the problem appears in volume 5 of *Testimonies for the Church,* pages 692 through 696. It can profitably be examined by all readers of Ellen White's writings: "Beware," she says, "how you give credence to such reports" (p. 694). She concludes her discussion of the topic with the following words: "To all who have a desire for truth I would say: Do not give credence to unauthenticated reports as to what Sister White has done or said or written. If you desire to know what the Lord has revealed through her, read her published works. . . . Do not eagerly catch up and report rumors as to what she has said" (p. 696).

In a similar vein W. C. White offered the following advice in 1904: "Let everyone who hears such rumors say: 'I am advised to pay no attention to such reports, and I cannot accept this as a statement of Sister White, unless you show it to me in writing, with her signature. Then I will send it to her, and ask if it is correct'" (W. C. White to W. S. Sadler, Jan. 20, 1904).

W. C. White, of course, was talking about her unpublished letters rather than her published books and articles, but the idea is clear. And while we can no longer "send it to her" for her verification, we can contact the White Estate office at General Conference headquarters or visit the nearest White Estate Research Center to verify the authenticity of a statement or to inquire about other questions we might have. Too many people fail to take advantage of the services available to them via phone, the mail, or fax machine.

An issue closely related to the problem of statements falsely attributed to Ellen White is the question of prophetic extensions of Ellen White. Some people over the years have used Ellen White statements to imply that her strong endorsement of certain writers or ministers granted to their works or ideas some sort of prophetic authority.

As a result, when some have read that the "angels of heaven were by his [Martin Luther's] side, and rays of light from the throne of God revealed the treasures of truth to his understanding" (GC 122), they came to believe that his ideas were as inspired as those of a prophet. While Ellen White certainly was arguing that God used Luther and the angels guided him in his general work, it would be an error to infer that she agreed with all of his theology.

A similar case is that of William Miller. Ellen White wrote of him that "God sent His angel to move upon the heart of a farmer who had not believed the Bible, to lead him to search the prophecies. Angels of God repeatedly visited that chosen one, to guide his mind and open to his understanding prophecies which had ever been dark to God's people" (EW 229). Such words, while implying Ellen White's prophetic endorsement of Miller's general understanding, must not be interpreted to mean that she believed he was correct in all things. For example, she most certainly differed with Miller on the identity of the sanctuary to be cleansed at the end of the 2300 days.

It is a point of interest that people have seen the leaders on both sides of the Seventh-day Adventist struggle at Minneapolis in 1888 as extensions of Ellen White's prophetic authority. Thus some, hearing that Ellen White had purportedly stated that the heavenly angels had helped Uriah Smith in his work of writing *Daniel and the Revelation,* came to treat the book as almost being inspired and thus not subject to revision. After all, hadn't she recommended "that that book should go everywhere" (letter 25a 1889)? And hadn't she penned that *"Thoughts on Daniel and the Revelation, The Great Controversy,* and *Patriarchs and Prophets* . . . contain the very message the people must have, the special light God had given His people. The angels of God would prepare the way for these books in the hearts of the people" (CM 123, 124)?

Such sentiments led to what W. C. White called the "infallibility doctrine" regarding Smith's influential treatment of the prophecies (W. C. White to J. H. Waggoner, Feb. 27, 1889) and prompted many to hold that Smith's work should not be revised, since Ellen White had given it her strong endorsement. Thus some came to consider Smith's treatment of Daniel and Revelation as a prophetic extension of Ellen White. They implied that we should not question or alter Smith's ideas, because they had the sanction of the prophetic gift.

Others employ the same logic for the teachings of A. T. Jones and E. J. Waggoner, Smith's opponents at the 1888 General Conference session. Because Ellen White repeatedly endorsed the two men and said in unmistakable terms that God had sent them and that they had "a most precious message" (TM 91) for the Adventist Church, some have seen her as almost giving their theology a total endorsement up through about 1896. Thus Waggoner and Jones have also been seen as candidates for prophetic extension.

But, as in the cases of Luther, Miller, and Smith, we must be careful here. For one thing, Mrs. White needed to make strong statements endorsing Jones and Waggoner's message if they were to get any hearing, since the General Conference leadership was unjustly opposed to them. Second, they had a message about Jesus and salvation by faith that the denomination desperately needed. And third, Ellen White several times claimed that she did not agree with all of their theology. For example, in November 1888 she told the assembled General Conference delegates that "some interpretations of Scripture given by Dr. Waggoner I do not regard as correct" (1888 Materials 164). However, she did not specify where she agreed or disagreed with him.

In summary, Ellen White has no prophetic extensions. To use her writings to create such extensions can be misleading. If people really want to see what she believed and taught, they should follow her advice: "If you desire to know what the Lord has revealed through her, read her published works" (5T 696).

Chapter Twenty

A Few More
Principles of Interpretation

For the past 14 chapters we have examined basic principles of interpretation for Ellen White's writings. Before moving away from that part of our study, we need to look briefly at a few additional helpful points.

The first is that we should be aware that both the Bible writers and Ellen White use hyperbole and other figures of speech from time to time. Thus the apostle John can write that "there are also many other things which Jesus did, the which, if they should be written every one, I suppose that even the world itself could not contain the books that should be written" (John 21:25). Again in Hebrews 11:13 we read that "these *all* died in faith, not having received the promises," when obviously *not all* had died, since Enoch is one of those enumerated (verse 5). In a similar manner, the book of Daniel employs figures of speech when it talks about the furnace being seven times hotter (Dan. 3:19) and the Hebrew worthies being 10 times better (Dan. 1:20) than the other young men questioned by Nebuchadnezzar. Those figures of speech indicate that it was much hotter and that the Hebrew young men were definitely superior, but they are not talking about IQ percentages or measurable temperatures.

Of course, some always end up with fanatical interpretations because they refuse to recognize that the Bible writers use figures of speech. In that class are those who disgusted Martin Luther when he found old folks playing hoops in the street because the Gospel said that except you become as little children, you cannot enter the kingdom of heaven. The same thing happened in post-Disappointment Adventism among those who dispensed with the use of knives and forks and crawled around town to do their shopping in order to demonstrate that they were like little children and thus a part of the kingdom. Certain types of fanaticism refuse to recognize figures of speech in either the Bible or Ellen White's writings.

A study of her comments on what is the highest human calling helps us see Ellen White's use of superlatives as a literary device to encourage people to be faithful to their callings and talents, no matter what they might be. Thus she could say that teachers and mothers have the most important work in the world. But she could also write in various places that physicians, ministers, and colporteurs also have the most important work. She even stated that the cook who prepared the meals at Battle Creek College held the position of "first" importance within the institution (FE 226). In such statements she isn't so much setting forth a calculus as to which task is truly the *most* valuable as she is seeking to encourage various people to do their best by highlighting the importance of using their personal talents for God's glory. Of course, if people so desire, they can pit the various statements against one another, but that appears to be a fruitless exercise.

Ellen White was also fond of using such phrases as 1 in 20 (five times), 10 in 100 (one time), 1 in 50 (one time), and 1 in 100 (23 times). Once again these seem to be figures of speech rather than exact statements of proportion. She never, for example, says 2 out of 13 or 1 in 18.

Failure to take into account figures of speech can make us overly rigid (or exacting) in reading Ellen White and the Bible. There have been some serious incidents in church history when some rejected the idea that the Bible uses figures of speech and consequently plucked out their right eye, cut off their right hand, or emasculated themselves when faced with certain temptations.

And the pagans in Rome jumped to the conclusion that Christians were cannibals, since they "ate" the flesh and "drank" the blood of Jesus behind closed doors. But we do not have to arrive at such conclusions when we realize that God's prophets use figures of speech in their writings.

A second helpful principle is that we should interpret inspired language according to its obvious meaning unless it employs symbols or figures (see GC 599). Some people come up with fantastic conclusions because they read symbolic ideas into places that are straightforward prose.

Closely related to that point is a third principle of interpretation, which holds that the Bible and the writings of Ellen White explain themselves. Thus Ellen White writes that "the Bible is its own expositor. One passage will prove to be a key that will unlock other passages, and in this way light will be shed upon the hidden meaning of the word. By comparing different texts treating on the same subject, viewing their bearing on every side, the true meaning of the Scriptures will be made evident" (FE 187). She has a similar thing to say of her own works. Thus we read that "the testimonies themselves will be the key that will explain the messages given, as scripture is explained by scripture" (1SM 42).

That principle is especially helpful when we come across statements that seem to be obscure. It generally helps to turn to other passages on the same topic. Those statements often approach the subject from a different angle and sometimes provide information or insights that clear up the obscurity of the first statement.

Also, it is important to let Ellen White's general counsel on a topic supply some of the conceptual framework for counsel given to a specific individual. Remember, be wary of an interpretation of any statement that seems out of harmony with the general tenor of Ellen White's writings or the counsel of the Bible. Such apparently aberrant interpretations generally indicate the need for further study on the topic.

A fourth principle is that we should be wary of any interpretations of Ellen White or the Bible that seem to be "new" or unique. We noted earlier in this volume that some types of personality are always looking for something new, even when they haven't mastered the central truths of already established light. Such students often fly off on an independent tangent. Working closely with those of experience with the Bible and Ellen White's writings can at times save us from much grief. "You must," wrote Ellen White to one individual in 1863, "restrain the disposition within you of being original. You must lean upon the faith of the body or you will mar the work of God, and injure the truth. No new ideas should be advocated by preachers or people upon their own responsibility. All new ideas should be thoroughly investigated and decided upon. If there is any weight in them they should be adopted by the body; if not, rejected" (letter 8, 1863).

In another connection Mrs. White penned: "Let none be self-confident, as though God had given them special light above their brethren. Christ is represented as dwelling in His people. . . .

"That which Brother D calls light is apparently harmless; it does not look as though anyone could be injured by it. But, brethren, it is Satan's device, his entering wedge. This has been tried again and again. One accepts some new and original idea which does not seem to conflict with the truth. He talks of it and dwells upon it until it seems to him to be clothed with beauty and importance, for Satan has power to give this false appearance. At last it becomes the all-absorbing theme, the one great truth around which everything centers. . . .

"The only safety for any of us is in receiving no new doctrine, no new interpretation of the Scriptures [the same could be said of Ellen White's writings], without first submitting it to brethren of experience. Lay it before them in a humble, teachable spirit, with earnest prayer; and if they see no light in it, yield to their judgment; for 'in the multitude of counselors there is safety'" (5T 291-293). If we more often followed that advice, it would prevent a great deal of confusion in the Adventist Church and in the lives of many of Ellen White's readers.

A final point of interpretation that we will discuss is that one should never build an argument from silence. That is, we must not assume that something is true because we are certain that

Ellen White would have said something on the topic if she had been against it (or for it). For example, even though she knew of J. H. Kellogg's pantheism for years, she said nothing about his views. Yet because she did not make an issue on the topic during the late 1890s or early 1900s, he assumed that she agreed with him. That conclusion, as Kellogg eventually discovered, was far from the truth.

A study of Adventist history demonstrates, contrary to the general impression of many, that Mrs. White was frequently silent on even important issues. She often refrained from speaking until she had a definite word from the Lord on a subject. Thus she did not comment for a long period of time on the potentially destructive situation of Anna Rice Phillips, who claimed to be a prophet in the early 1890s. On November 1, 1893, she wrote: "Letters have come to me presenting before me the case of Sister Phillips, and inquiries have been made to me [concerning] what I thought of the matter. I have not felt called out to encourage or condemn so long as I had no special light in reference to this case. . . . I decided to let the matter develop" (letter 54 1893).

It is never safe to base an argument on silence. We must always work with what Ellen White has written, and even then we must be sure to follow sound principles of interpretation.

For the greater portion of this book we have been examining principles of interpreting Ellen White's writings. We will now turn to the next important step in our reading of her writings—the process of applying our findings. That will be the subject of our last two chapters as we consider their application both to ourselves and to others.

Principles of
Application

Chapter Twenty-one

Applying the Counsel to My Life: A Question of Faithfulness

W hether or not my life is spared," Ellen White wrote in 1907, "my writings will constantly speak, and their work will go forward as long as time shall last" (1SM 55). And they continue to do so. Their primary function, however, is not to speak in general terms but to address my life, my situation, my heart. My first responsibility is not to seek to apply Ellen White's counsel to the lives of others, but to examine my life to see how her writings can enrich it.

"I was," we read, ". . . directed to bring out general principles, in speaking and in writing, and at the same time specify the dangers, errors, and sins of some individuals, that all might be warned, reproved, and counseled. I saw that all should search their own hearts and lives closely to see if they had not made the same mistakes for which others were corrected and if the warnings given for others did not apply to their own cases. If so, they should feel that the counsel and reproofs were given especially for them and should make as practical an application of them as though they were especially addressed to themselves" (2T 687).

Again we read, "Since the warning and instruction given in testimony for individual cases applied with equal force to many others who had not been specially pointed out in this manner, it seemed to be my duty to publish the personal testimonies for the benefit of the church" (5T 658, 659). "If one is reproved for a special wrong, brethren and sisters should carefully examine themselves to see wherein they have failed and wherein they have been guilty of the same sin. . . . In rebuking the wrongs of one, He designs to correct many" (2T 112).

What Ellen White has said about rebukes and warnings in the previous quotations also holds true for promises and blessings. Both in the Bible and in the Ellen White writings God has a message for His people. It is a message calculated to help us in every way, that we might not only have a happier, healthier, saner life on this earth but that we might also be guided to the world made new.

The point to remember is that God's messages are for *me*. My first task is to apply them to my personal life.

But, I must admit, sometimes I don't like what God has to say. Or at times I like part of a message but not other segments. If that is true, I am then in the company of some well-known Adventists. Ellen White spoke to that situation in her own day. "When it suits your purpose," she wrote to one person in 1891, "you treat the Testimonies as if you believed them, quoting from them to strengthen any statement you wish to have prevail. But how is it when light is given to correct your errors? Do you then accept the light? When the Testimonies speak contrary to your ideas, you treat them very lightly" (1SM 43).

On another occasion she referred to those "who will dare to draw the line in this matter and say, this portion which pleases me is from God, but that portion which points out and condemns my course of conduct is from Sister White alone, and bears not the holy signet. You have in this way virtually rejected the whole of the messages, which God in His tender, pitying love has sent to you to save you from moral ruin" (3SM 69).

We need to be honest with ourselves. Either God has spoken through Mrs. White or He hasn't. If He has, then it behooves us to be as honest with ourselves as possible as we seek to apply the counsel in her writings. But we ought to be consistent. We shouldn't be like those she wrote about in 1863 who "profess to believe the testimony borne" and who "do harm by making them an iron rule" for others but "fail to carry them out themselves" (1T 369).

"Do not pick flaws any more," Ellen White told a group of Adventist leaders in 1901. "O, I see enough buzzards, and I see enough vultures that are trying and watching for dead bodies; but we . . . want nothing of that. We want no picking and picking and picking of flaws in others. Attend to Number One, and you have got all that you have got to do. If you attend to Number One, and if you will purify your souls by obeying the truth, you will have something to impart, you will have a power to give to others. God help you! I beseech of him to help you, every one of you, and to help me" (MS 43a, 1901).

That is excellent advice. For too long have some of the readers of Ellen White played the part of buzzards and vultures in feeding upon the faults and shortcomings of others and the church. Our primary task is to examine not others but ourselves.

In this connection I must ask myself why I read Ellen White's writings. I need to be frank with myself as to my focus and motivation. Too often I find myself saying "That is an excellent piece of advice for my wife or my pastor or my neighbor," when all the while God wants me to say in my heart, "That is just the counsel I need, since I am struggling in that area."

In short, I need to read in such a way that God is able to speak to my heart. I must put my burden to straighten out everybody else on the shelf and just let God have His way in my life. And I need to pray for clear eyesight so that I will not only be able to read with honesty but that I will also be able to apply the counsel in a meaningful and helpful way to my daily life. That takes not only honesty and dedication but also the power of God's Holy Spirit.

Chapter Twenty-two

Applying Counsel to Others:
A Question of Loving Care

J
udge not, that you be not judged. . . . Why do you see the *speck* that is in your brother's eye, but do not notice the *log* that is in your own eye? . . . First take the log out of your own eye, and then you will see clearly to take the speck out of your brother's eye" (Matt. 7:1-5, RSV).

Eye surgery is a delicate task, requiring the greatest tenderness and love. We desire people to be tender to us, and the golden rule tells us that we *must* be tender to them.

According to the Sermon on the Mount and what we have read in the previous chapter, there does come a time for helping others to see truth in a fuller way, but that time arrives only after our own hearts have been softened by insights into our own weaknesses and by our gratitude to God for rescuing us from the pit of despair.

One of the great problems facing the church down through history, however, has been those who have never been to the pit of despair. Such "saints" generally think quite highly of their spiritual accomplishments and feel justified in condemning others who have not reached their "high" level. They have a pedigree of long standing—they partake of the spirit of the Pharisees.

Ellen White spent her entire life fighting that spirit. She even refused to publish "some things which are all truth . . . because I fear that some would take advantage of them to hurt others" (letter 32, 1901).

Even though she had strong convictions in many areas of life, she gave people (including those who lived with her) freedom to make their own choices. Thus, for example, she wrote in regard to health reform that "the other members of my family do not eat the same things that I do. I do not hold myself up as a criterion for them. I leave each one to follow his own ideas as to what is best for him. I bind no one else's conscience by my own. One person cannot be a criterion for another in the matter of eating. It is impossible to make one rule for all to follow" (CD 491; cf. MH 320; 3SM 294).

But not all of Mrs. White's supposed followers have been as gracious as she. As a result, she penned that *"it is the desire and plan of Satan to bring in among us those who will go to great extremes*—people of narrow minds, who are critical and sharp, and very tenacious in holding their own conceptions of what the truth means. *They will be exacting, and will seek to enforce rigorous duties, and go to great lengths in matters of minor importance, while they neglect the weightier matters of the law—judgment and mercy and the love of God"* (MM 269; italics supplied).

Satan has had those who have agitated extremism to the point of fanaticism in many areas in Adventism. But perhaps (as the many quotations in this chapter will demonstrate) no area has found so many enthusiasts for extremism as health reform. "My brother," she penned to one advocate, "you are not to make a test for the people of God, upon the question of diet; for they will lose confidence in teachings that are strained to the farthest point of extension. The Lord desires His people to be sound on every point in health reform, but we must not go to extremes" (CD 205). Again she wrote that we "should be careful not to urge even right ideas unduly" *(ibid.* 398).

Perhaps the ultimate misunderstanding of Ellen White's counsel appeared in the *Reformation Herald* of January-March 1991. The editor, in an article entitled "Flesh Eating in the Last Days," collected a large number of statements about items that Ellen White claimed should not be made into tests, including such areas as diet, dress reform, flesh-eating, raising pigs, and so on.

He recognized the breadth of her statements, but then went on to argue that times had changed and that now all these things were indeed tests. "The tolerant standards adopted by the church in the days of the pioneers," he pontificated, "must be left behind as a thing of the past, and much higher standards must be attained today. . . . Since the 'no-test' counsels of Sister White can be taken only as temporary tolerance measures, and not as permanent laws, we deal with meat eating the way we deal with *other sins*. We tell the person involved that if he contemplates membership in the Reform Movement he must sacrifice his idol. . . . Perverted appetite, which includes meat eating, is sin" (italics supplied).

So much for the New Testament view on the topic (see, for example, Rom. 14:17; John 21:9-12), and Ellen White's many moderating remarks. Such people push for the most extreme interpretation.

But, some will undoubtedly argue, wouldn't Ellen White urge such a course if she were alive today? In responding to that question, we must consider several points. The first is that she isn't alive. Thus all we have of her counsel is what she has written. Anything beyond that is human speculation. Second, she consistently opposed those who mixed their reason in with her counsel to extend her ideas to extremes. Third, all that she has written leads away from the course of action recommended above by certain extremist elements.

Let's let Mrs. White speak for herself. "You, or any other deluded person," she penned, "could arrange . . . certain scriptures [the same principle applies for Ellen White quotations] of great force, and appl[y] them according to your own ideas. Any man could misinterpret and misapply God's Word, denouncing people and things, and then take the position that those who refused to receive his message had rejected the message of God, and decided their destiny for eternity" (1SM 44).

"Do not," she said on another occasion, "when referring to the Testimonies, feel it your duty to drive them home. In reading them, be sure not to mix in your filling of words; for this makes it impossible for the hearers to distinguish between the word of the Lord to them and your words" (GW 374). The mixing in of human words to extend the counsel, along with failing to take the full literary/historical context into consideration, has been at the heart of a great deal of the fanaticism of those who have pushed Ellen White's counsel beyond its original intent.

Such extremism tends to discourage faithful believers. "I saw," Mrs. White commented, "that many have taken advantage of what God has shown in regard to the sins and wrongs of others. They have taken the *extreme meaning* of what has been shown in vision, and then have pressed it until it has had a tendency to weaken the faith of many in what God has shown, and also to discourage and dishearten the church" (1T 166; italics supplied).

Repeatedly Ellen White asserted that such extremists lack the love of God and do more harm than good. "There are many," she noted in 1889, "whose religion consists in criticising habits of dress and manners. They want to bring every one to their own measure. . . . *They have lost the love of God out of their hearts; but they think they have a spirit of discernment.* They think it is their prerogative to criticise, and pronounce judgment; but they should repent of their error, and turn away from their sins. . . . Let us love one another. . . . Let us look upon the light that abides for us in Jesus. Let us remember how forbearing and patient he was with the erring children of men. We should be in a wretched state if the God of heaven were like one of us, and treated us as we are inclined to treat one another" (RH Aug. 27, 1889; italics supplied).

One of the first signals indicating that someone is off a wholesome Christian course is when criticism regarding other people, the church, and so on begins to fill them. The spirit of Christ is one of sorrow, caring, and love rather than self-righteous criticism.

Perhaps the most forceful statement by Ellen White regarding those who wrongly use her writings is the following. Those with an interest in Mrs. White's writings would do well to read it in full in *Selected Messages,* book 3, pages 283-288. Because of its importance to our discussion, we will quote from it extensively.

"Statements are made," Ellen White observed, "that some are taking the light in the testimonies upon health reform and making it a test. They select statements made in regard to some articles of diet that are presented as objectionable—statements written in warning and instruction to certain individuals. . . . They dwell on these things and make them as strong as possible, weaving their own peculiar, objectionable traits of character in with these statements and carry them with great force, thus making them a test, and driving them where they do only harm.

"The meekness and lowliness of Christ is wanting. Moderation and caution are greatly needed, but they have not these desirable traits of character. They need the mold of God upon them. And such persons may take health reform and do great harm with it in prejudicing minds so that ears will be closed to the truth. . . .

"*We see those who will select from the testimonies the strongest expressions and, without bringing in or making any account of the circumstances under which the cautions and warnings are given, make them of force in every case.* Thus they produce unhealthy impressions upon the minds of the people. *There are always those who are ready to grasp anything of a character which they can use to rein up people to a close, severe test, and who will work elements of their own characters into the reforms. . . . They will go at the work, making a raid upon the people.* Picking out some things in the testimonies they drive them upon every one, and disgust rather than win souls. They make divisions when they might and should make peace. . . .

"*Let the testimonies speak for themselves. Let not individuals gather up the very strongest statements, given for individuals and families, and drive these things.*" To the contrary, when "their own hearts [are] softened and subdued by the grace of Christ," when "their own spirits [are] humble and full of the milk of human kindness, they will not create prejudice, neither will they cause dissension and weaken the churches" (3SM 285-287; italics supplied).

W. C. White had to deal with many who sought to use the "straight testimony" of Ellen White as a ramrod. In 1919 he wrote about one group who was preparing to publish an independent compilation. "The work of some members of this group," he penned, "appeared to me like that of men who were forging steel rules with which to measure their brethren, and some were quite proficient in telling wherein Elder Daniells [the General Conference president] was short, wherein Elder Knox [the General Conference treasurer] failed to meet the standard, and wherein George Thompson was at fault. As I met and conversed with them I did not undertake to prove that they were wrong in their assertions that other men were wrong but I tried to show them that they would not correct the wrong by the methods they were following. . . .

"I did not feel that anything would be gained by meeting these men in a combative way and instead of arguing the matter with them and trying to show them wherein it was wrong I told them that mother, if she were living, would be greatly grieved to have done that which they were planning to do" (W. C. White to D. E. Robinson, July 27, 1919).

The message of this chapter should be clear. We need to be careful in using the counsel of Ellen White in both how we read and interpret it and how we apply it. Any application must be done in good sense and Christian love and in a spirit of humility.

We will close this study with a quotation from M. L. Andreasen, a leading Adventist for much of the first half of the twentieth century: "I believe, friends, that we ought to give heed to the messages God has given [through Ellen White], apply them to ourselves and not judge others. Oh, the intolerance of some who think they are right! Let them be right. But do not judge others.

"I believe we have come to the time when Sister White must be given a definite place in our teaching. We must not place her above the Bible, nor must we reject her. We must use the sense God has given us. . . . Be cautious of your application and assertions. Never say that because someone disagrees with you that he does not believe the *Testimonies*. He may not believe your interpretation of them, but still he may believe them as fully as you do, and have a more balanced view" (M. L. Andreasen, unpublished MS, Nov. 30,

1948). That statement, as one thinks about it in the context of what we have discussed in this book, is worth contemplating.

We have reached the end of this book, but hopefully we have also come to the beginning of a richer reading of God's counsel to His end-time people. It is one thing to read this book, but quite another to apply the principles discussed in it to our reading and to our lives. God has a blessing in store for each of us as we read both the Bible and Ellen White's writings with expanded understanding and renewed dedication.

Praise God for all His blessings!

Meeting Ellen White

by George R. Knight

George R. Knight helps readers understand and appreciate the fascinating life and role of Ellen White.

Part one presents a concise biographical overview of her life. Part two introduces you to both her published and unpublished writings, showing the major categories of her counsel to the church. Part three explores seven major themes that run through everything she wrote. Paperback, US$8.99, Cdn$12.99.

This Review and Herald book is available at all ABC Christian bookstores (1-800-765-6955) and other Christian bookstores. Prices and availability subject to change. Add GST in Canada.